S0-BOG-386

Mobil
Travel Guide®

LUXURY
DRIVES

ACKNOWLEDGMENTS

We gratefully acknowledge the help of our representatives for their efficient and perceptive inspections of the lodging and dining establishments listed, the establishments' proprietors for their cooperation in showing their facilities and providing information about them, and the many users of previous editions who have taken the time to share their experiences. Mobil Travel Guide is also grateful to all the talented writers who contributed entries to this book.

Front cover images:
Road to Hana: ©istockphoto.com/Linda Blair; Fraser Island, Australia: ©istockphoto.com/Chee-Onn Leong; "Leaf Looker" Season in the Mountains: ©istockphoto.com/Forest Woodward

All illustrated maps: © Jennifer Thermes

The information contained herein is derived from a variety of third-party sources. Although every effort has been made to verify the information obtained from such sources, the publisher assumes no responsibility for inconsistencies or inaccuracies in the data or liability for any damages of any type arising from errors or omissions.

Neither the editors nor the publisher assume responsibility for the services provided by any business listed in this guide or for any loss, damage or disruption in your travel for any reason.

ISBN: 9-780841-60745-3   Manufactured in Canada.
10 9 8 7 6 5 4 3 2 1

TABLE OF CONTENTS

WRITTEN IN THE STARS

Because your time is precious and the travel world is ever-changing, having accurate travel information when you hit the road is essential. Mobil Travel Guide has provided the most trusted advice to travelers for more than 50 years.

The Mobil Corporation (known as Exxon Mobil Corporation since a 1999 merger) launched the Mobil Travel Guide books in 1958 following the introduction of the U.S. interstate highway system two years earlier. The first edition covered only five Southwestern states. Since then, our books have become the premier travel guides in North America, covering all 50 states and Canada. Recently, we've added international destinations, expanding the Mobil Travel Guide brand around the world.

Today, the concept of a "five star" experience is one that permeates the collective consciousness, but is one that originated with Mobil. Mobil Travel Guide created its star rating system to give travelers an easy to recognize quality scale for choosing where to stay and dine. Only Mobil's star ratings deliver a rigorously tested formula for determining if a hotel, restaurant or spa is as luxurious as its owners claim. Our rating system is the oldest and most respected in North America, and most hoteliers, restaurateurs and industry insiders understand the prestige and benefits that come with receiving a Mobil Star rating.

The Mobil Travel Guide process of rating each establishment includes unannouced facility inspections, incognito service evaluations and a review of unsolicited comments from the general public.

We inpsect more than 500 attributes at each property we visit, from cleanliness, to the condition of the rooms and public spaces, to employee attitude and courtesy. All are evaluated to produce a mathematically derived score, which is then blended with other elements to form an overall score. It's a system that rewards those properties that strive for and achieve excellence each year. And the very best properties raise the bar for those that wish to compete with them.

Only facilities that meet our standards earn the privilege of being listed in the guide. Properties are continuously updated, and deteriorating, poorly managed establishments are removed. We wouldn't recommend that you visit a hotel, restaurant or spa that we wouldn't want to visit ourselves.

If any aspect of your accommodation, dining, spa or sightseeing experience motivates you to comment, please contact us at Mobil Travel Guide, 200 W. Madison St., Suite 3950, Chicago, IL 60606, or send an email to info@mobiltravelguide.com. Happy travels.

STAR RATINGS

HOTELS

Whether you're looking for the ultimate in luxury or the best bang for your travel buck, we have a hotel recommendation for you. To help you pinpoint properties that meet your needs, Mobil Travel Guide classifies each lodging by type according to the following characteristics.

★★★★★The Mobil Five-Star hotel provides consistently superlative service in an exceptionally distinctive luxury environment. Attention to detail is evident throughout the hotel, resort or inn, from bed linens to staff uniforms.

★★★★The Mobil Four-Star hotel provides a luxury experience with expanded amenities in a distinctive environment. Services may include automatic turndown service, 24-hour room service and valet parking.

★★★The Mobil Three-Star hotel is well appointed, with a full-service restaurant and expanded amenities, such as a fitness center, golf course, tennis courts, 24-hour room service and optional turndown service.

★★The Mobil Two-Star hotel is considered a clean, comfortable and reliable establishment that has expanded amenities, such as a full-service restaurant.

★The Mobil One-Star lodging is a limited-service hotel, motel or inn that is considered a clean, comfortable and reliable establishment.

Recommended A Mobil-recommended property is a reliable, standout property new to our guides at press time that are simply listed in our pages. Look for a Mobil star-rating for these properties in the future.

For every property, we also provide pricing information. The pricing categories break down as follows:

$ = Up to $150
$$ = $151-$250
$$$ = $251-$350
$$$$ = $351 and up

All prices quoted are accurate at the time of publication, however prices cannot be guaranteed.

RESTAURANTS

All Mobil Star-rated dining establishments listed in this book have a full kitchen and most offer table service.

★★★★★The Mobil Five-Star restaurant offers one of few flawless dining experiences in the country. These establishments consistently provide their guests with exceptional food, superlative service, elegant décor and exquisite presentations of each detail surrounding a meal.

★★★★The Mobil Four-Star restaurant provides professional service, distinctive presentations and wonderful food.

★★★The Mobil Three-Star restaurant has good food, warm and skillful service and enjoyable décor.

★★The Mobil Two-Star restaurant serves fresh food in a clean setting with efficient service. Value is considered in this category, as is family friendliness.

★The Mobil One-Star restaurant provides a distinctive experience through culinary specialty, local flair or individual atmosphere.

Because menu prices can fluctuate, we list a pricing category rather than specific prices. The pricing categories are defined as follows, per diner, and assume that you order an appetizer or dessert, an entrée and one drink:

$ = $15 and under
$$ = $16-$35
$$$ = $36-$85
$$$$ = $86 and up

SPAS

Mobil Travel Guide's spa ratings are based on objective evaluations of more than 450 attributes. Approximately half of these criteria assess basic expectations, such as staff courtesy, the technical proficiency and skill of the employees and whether the facility is maintained properly and hygienically. Several standards address issues that impact a guest's physical comfort and convenience, as well as the staff's ability to impart a sense of personalized service and anticipate clients' needs. Additional criteria measure the spa's ability to create a completely calming ambience

★★★★★The Mobil Five-Star spa provides consistently superlative service in an exceptionally distinctive luxury environment with extensive amenities. The staff at a Mobil Five-Star spa provides extraordinary service beyond the traditional spa experience, allowing guests to achieve the highest level of relaxation and pampering. A Mobil Five-Star spa offers an extensive array of treatments, often incorporating international themes and products. Attention to detail is evident throughout the spa, from arrival to departure.

★★★★The Mobil Four-Star spa provides a luxurious experience with expanded amenities in an elegant and serene environment. Throughout the spa facility, guests experience personalized service. Amenities might include, but are not limited to, single-sex relaxation rooms where guests wait for their treatments, plunge pools and whirlpools in both men's and women's locker rooms, and an array of treatments, including a selection of massages, body therapies, facials and a variety of salon services.

★★★The Mobil Three-Star spa is physically well appointed and has a full complement of staff.

INTRODUCTION

Maybe you're looking to get out of the city for a long weekend. Or catch the buzz in wine country during the annual harvest. Perhaps you're yearning to cruise down the scenic Pacific Coast Highway or discover just how luxurious a rural country inn can be.

Wherever your starting point, whatever your timeframe, we've got your destinations covered (and your driving directions, too). In this guide, we tell you the best routes to take to avoid that pesky rush-hour traffic, the top hotels to recoup after a long day behind the wheel and the restaurants that will leave you wishing they could deliver all the way back home.

Experience the pleasures of Southern hospitality on a journey from the storied streets of Savannah to the church steeples of Charleston, and gain a history of low country cuisine along the way. Or greet our friendly neighbors to the north with an "eh" on a drive from Seattle to picturesque Vancouver, and realize why the city is often considered the shopping capital of Canada. We'll tell you the most delicious thing to do in Whistler (hint: it's not skiing) and where you must whip out your camera for magnificent shots of the majestic Rockies.

California's sunny disposition means it's always a good time to hit the road, which is why we've covered six of the state's most scenic routes with one-of-a-kind destinations, including La Jolla's The Lodge at Torrey Pines and the celebrated Chateau du Sureau in Oakhurst. If winding your way through cliff-side roads amidst crashing surf and untouched wilderness is more your thing, we'll show you how to drive to Big Sur in style.

Treat yourself to the serenity of Blackberry Farm, a relatively undiscovered 4,200-acre gem in the foothills of the Great Smoky Mountains, only a few hours from the country music mecca of Nashville. Or stroll the cliff walk of Newport, Rhode Island at dusk, with mansion after mansion hinting at a bygone era of opulence on one side and the sun dipping into the ocean on the other.

Road trips aren't just for summer weekend getaways and cross-country family escapades. Whether it's to enjoy the fall foliage, hit the best slopes in winter, seek out the first blooms of spring or spend the summer beach-hopping, there's always time for a luxury drive. A willing and able co-pilot (though we'll settle for a spot in the glove box), this guide will point you in the right direction, so all you have to do is ride off into the sunset.

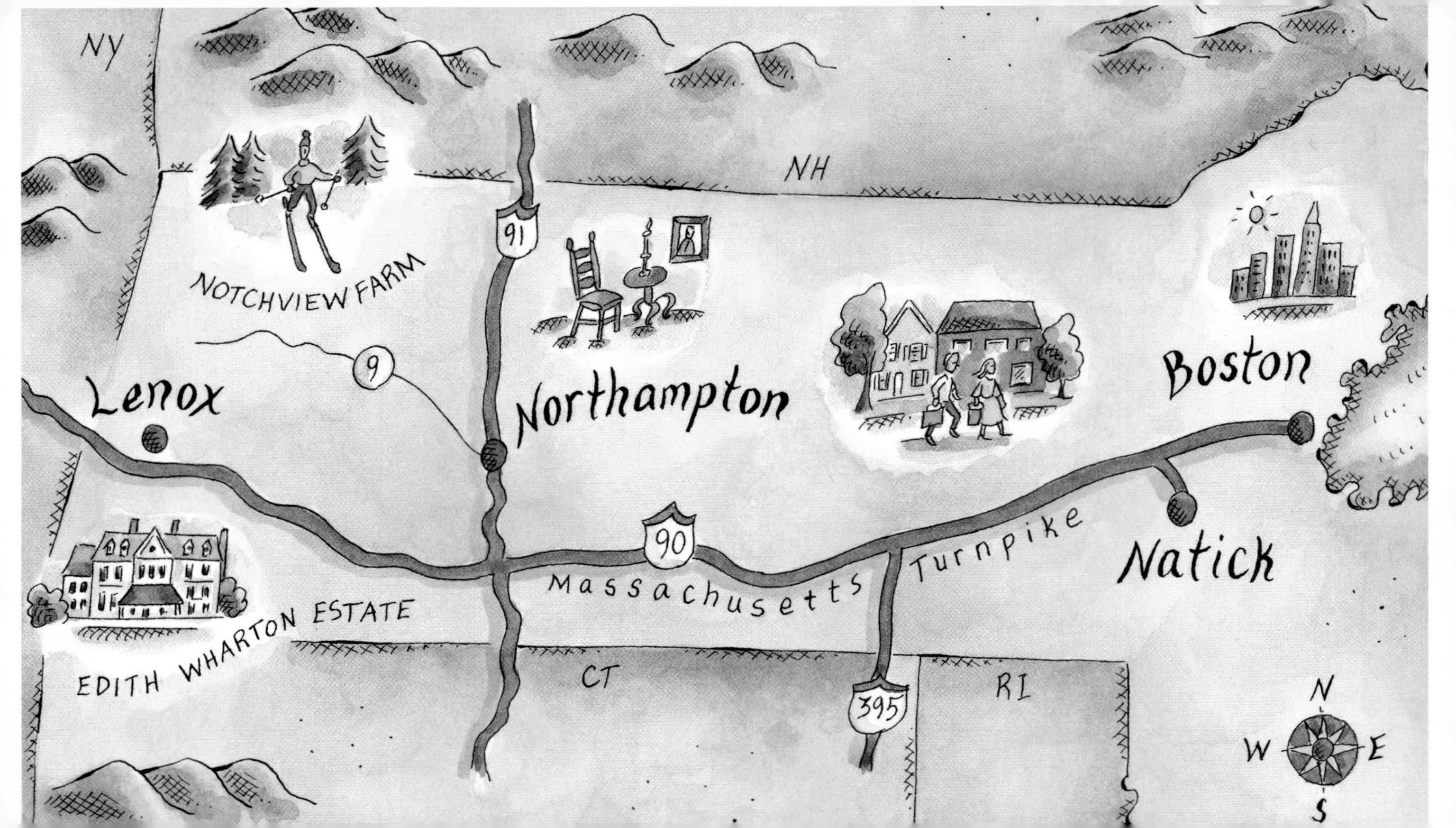
NY
NH
NOTCHVIEW FARM
91
9
Lenox
Northampton
Boston
90
Natick
Massachusetts Turnpike
EDITH WHARTON ESTATE
CT
395
RI
N
W
E
S

CHAPTER 1
BOSTON TO THE BERKSHIRES

From the center of Boston, there are about a hundred directions in which to go for a leisurely weekend escape. But no drive offers the scenic and cultural riches like the one that leads from Boston to the Berkshires. Whether you want to view some breathtaking foliage or watch a wintry landscape slide by, the 120 miles of highway and back roads here offer amazing views of the state's central valleys. What's more, the end is truly the reward—postcard-perfect towns, bistros serving up gourmet (and often organic) food, world-class arts and theater, and incredible inns to rest your head when you pull off the road. When it's time to turn back to Boston, take your time meandering down the narrow back roads. There's no need to hurry home.

starting out

Explore Boston from one of the city's Five Star hotels. The **Four Seasons Hotel Boston** (*200 Boylston St., Boston, 617-338-4400, 800-330-3442; www.fourseasons.com*) has guest rooms that overlook the Public Garden and Boston Common. The **Boston Harbor Hotel** (*70 Rowes Wharf, Boston, 617-439-7000, 800-752-7077; www.bhh.com*) is another great choice for its idyllic waterfront location (it's worth paying extra for a room with a view) and richly colored rooms. In the summer, live music, dancing and an alfresco movie night take place on the outdoor patio.

drive

If you're heading west out of Boston, especially at the beginning of a weekend, you'll wrestle with the fits and starts of outbound traffic no matter which road you take. The Massachuestts Turnpike (Interstate 90) tends to offer the quickest escape for the first part of the trip, but once you get to Worcester, you can slow down and get a more scenic view along Route 9.

Boston Harbor ▪ Boston Harbor Hotel ▪ Four Seasons Hotel Boston ▪ Garden at the Mount

It runs north of the main highway and intersects with dozens of picturesque town centers. Starting out on the Mass Pike (or "the Pike" as the locals lovingly call it), you're pointed due west, which means you might be rewarded with a glimpse of the sunset, especially after turning the bend at exit 14/15 for Interstate 95. That's when the road's long, flat stretches open up to views of the state's central hills and beyond. A few sloping turns and flat straightaways will take you the 15 miles out of town (and most likely, traffic) to exit 13 (Framingham/Natick). It's still fairly close to your starting point, but take some time to pull off here and visit the area's top new shopping spots.

see

Natick Collection

1245 Worcester St., Natick, 508-655-4800; www.natickmall.com

Locals won't call this a mall and neither should you. The shopping complex was revamped in late 2007 with the opening of a new wing. You can't miss it from the road: it resembles a giant, undulating wave. Head toward that entrance and you'll find valet parking along with access to the center's concierge shopping service. Inside, birch trees rise up from the nature-inspired first floor through the balconies above giving the whole space a serene, forest-in-the-winter appeal. The new space includes luxe retailers like Nordstrom, Danish design spot Stil and beauty apothecary Bluemercury. Pack up some sporting gear for the journey at Lululemon or a piece of monogrammed luggage at Louis Vuitton. A few well-respected restaurants from Boston, including Sel de la Terre, have opened locations here; stop by Sel's neighboring boulangerie to pick up a fresh-baked baguette or loaf of country sourdough and a foamy cappuccino to bolster yourself for the drive ahead. Monday-Saturday 10 a.m.-10 p.m., Sunday 11 a.m.-6 p.m.

drive

Jump back onto the Pike and head west toward Worcester. The long straightaways that get you there offer quiet treescapes occasionally interrupted by views of the Sudbury Reservoir. Take exit 10 to Interstate 290 North; get off at exit 17 (Route 9 Framingham/Ware) and turn left onto Belmont Street (follow signs for Route 9 West). As you continue on Route 9 past Worcester, more and more woodlands line the road, and you'll pass through towns like Leicester and Spencer, where you can take a quick detour through the hilly Luther Hill Park. Or stop by one of the local farm stands on the outskirts of Spencer, where the bins out front are loaded with corn, tomatoes and fresh flowers. In West Brookfield, you'll get a glimpse of a true small New England town where the original manicured square is surrounded by old Victorian houses. Church steeples dot the skyline. Just outside West Brookfield, the road turns into a twisty, shaded stretch with signs leading you from one town center to the next. These heavily wooded areas are interspersed with a few short stretches of farmland. You'll know you've arrived in Belchertown when you see the glassy waters of the Quabbin Reservoir peeking out between the trees on your right. The wildlife viewing area is worth a stop during warmer months.

About 50 miles west of Worcester, the small clusters of houses become a little tighter as the roadway leads you up a hilltop and into the town of Amherst. This storied Central Massachusetts town exudes academia. More than half its citizens are students (the other half might be professors), and its former inhabitants include such scholarly types as Eugene Field, Emily Dickinson, Robert Frost and Noah Webster. As the seat of Amherst College and the crown jewel of the University of Massachusetts system, this is a town filled with life, culture and

ERIC CARLE PICTURE BOOK MUSEUM

CHURCH IN LENOX

ideas. If you have time, be sure to stop at the picture book museum for a trip back to your childhood.

see
Eric Carle Picture Book Museum
125 W. Bay Road, Amherst, 413-658-1100; www.picturebookart.org
From the center of Amherst, take Route 116 south past the wooded neighborhoods that surround campus. Just past the entrance to Hampshire College, turn right onto Bay Road and the museum will be on your right. This 40,000-square-foot facility opened in 2002 as the first museum in the United States exclusively devoted to children's picture book art. Its founder, Eric Carle, has illustrated more than 70 picture books, including *The Very Hungry Caterpillar*, which has been published in more than 30 languages and has sold more than 22 million copies. Tuesday-Friday 10 a.m.-4 p.m., Saturday 10 a.m.-5 p.m., Sunday noon-5 p.m.

stop
A few miles west of Amherst and over the Connecticut River, you'll drive right into the heart of vibrant, artistic Northampton. Where Amherst feels academic and mature, Northampton has a more liberal vibe. It serves as the epicenter of schools like Amherst, Mount Holyoke, Smith, Hampshire and University of Massachusetts, whose student bodies fill the town with colorful characters. Thanks to Jonathan Edwards, a Puritan who was once regarded as the greatest preacher in New England, North-ampton was the scene of a frenzied religious revival movement in the early 18th century. However, the fervor had little lasting impact on the town, which is now full of first-class galleries, restaurants, antique shops, cafes, and up-to-date hotels and inns. The lawn of the courthouse acts as an outdoor sculpture garden and Main Street, which runs through the center of town, is a buzzing hub of activity. There are buskers, or street musicians, on just about every corner and it's not uncommon to find residents chatting over coffee (no matter what the weather) along the many park benches.

eat
Blue Heron
112 North Main St., Sunderland, 413-665-2102; www.blueherondining.com
Fifteen minutes north of Northamp-ton, in the quiet town of Sunderland, the Blue Heron sits in a white-steepled hall built in 1868; it was for-merly the town's municipal building. An open kitchen now lives where the clerks' offices once did and the interior has been refinished and painted in terra cotta, burnt amber and brown hues. At the entrance (from the back of the building), a gold-hued bar and lounge area is filled with low tables and there are banquet facilities on the second floor. Chef Deborah Snow offers a range of American cuisine made from regional cheeses, meats and fruits, and the staff is gracious and accommodating.
American menu. Dinner. Closed Mondays. Bar. Reservations recom-mended. $$$

The Green Bean
241 Main St., Northampton, 413-584-2326
This bright and jostling breakfast spot serves an all-organic menu of egg scrambles, sandwiches, pancakes and homemade granola. Wooden tables fill up fast so be prepared to wait (the line moves quickly). The coffee station is do-it-yourself, complete with a wrought-iron tree that holds the mugs. A café counter prepares lattes and espressos and there's also a kid-friendly menu.
Organic menu. Breakfast, lunch. $

see
Pinch
179 Main St., Northampton, 413-586-4509; www.pinchgallery.com
This colorful housewares shop and gallery has one of the best local arts and crafts collections in town. The eclectic mix of ceramics, tea sets, weavings, jewelry and ornaments make for good housewarming gifts. Local artists hand-design a number of the pottery pieces, and the photographs and prints that line the wall are also for sale.
Monday-Wednesday 10 a.m.-6 p.m., Thursday-Saturday 10 a.m.-9 p.m., Sunday 11 a.m.-5 p.m.

Smith College Museum of Art
Elm St., Northampton, 413-585-2760
This museum at the largest private women's liberal arts college in the United States has a fine collection of 19th and 20th century American and European art. Tuesday-Saturday 10 a.m.-4 p.m., Sunday noon-4 p.m., second Fridays 10 a.m.-8 p.m. (free after 4 p.m.); Closed Monday.

drive
Continue on Route 9 west and you'll travel past the rainbow-colored Victorians that sit on the outskirts of Northampton. The road follows the Mill River, which weaves back and forth underneath you, offering glimpses of the gurgling water along the way to the mill town of Williamsburg. Antique shops and sugar houses line the road, which starts a slow incline just

after the big red barn that houses the Williamsburg Blacksmith. The two-lane uphill climb is framed by rocky passes and stretches of farmland. At some points, towering spruce trees are all you can see and then a maple syrup stand pops into view. At the crest of the hill, just as you're entering Goshen, the other side of the hilly range spreads out before you. Red barns with white rooftops dot the landscape, which gives way to a sleepy, wooded pass as the road flattens out into ever-lengthening s-curves.

At Windsor, you're rewarded with a sign officially welcoming you into the Berkshires. It's a plateau that seems to float above the tree line. Even the massive spruces seem to shrink down to eye level and you become acutely aware of being 2,000 feet above sea level. This is one of the best viewing spots of the trip so take a few minutes to stop.

see
Notchview Farm
Route 9, Windsor, 413-684-0148; www.thetrustees.org
This 3,108-acre property, protected by the Trustees of the Reservation, is part of the Hoosac Range, which is really the southern portion of Vermont's Green Mountains. From the lookout point, there's an eagle-eye view of the sloping hills and valleys folding out beneath the range. With 25 miles of hiking trails and 19 miles of cross-country ski trails, it's worth visiting year-round. Open daily sunrise to sunset.

drive
From Windsor, stay on Route 9 until you hit Pittsfield (as the highway merges with other roadways, be sure to follow the signs for Route 9). Fuming factories and commercial areas give way to the larger municipal buildings at the center of town. A roundabout marks your departure from Route 9. Follow the signs toward Route 7/Lenox, making your way past a few cozy motels. Keep an eye out for the right hand turn onto Route 7A which leads into Lenox.

stop

Lenox is the Berkshires' most talked-about town, namely because of its proximity to such a vast concentration of cultural sites and events. Its name has become synonymous with rambling summer homes, many of which were built in the 19th century for the "banker baron" families of New York and beyond; they would stay from the moment the weather turned warm until the first cool breezes of fall swept through. Their homes are still in place in some cases, though many have been reopened as luxurious inns. The Boston Symphony Orchestra (*www.bso.org*) calls Tanglewood, the outdoor music venue located here, its summer base and the musical community of Lenox rallies with excitement for big names like John Williams and James Taylor who make appearances throughout the season. The literati, who have always found solace in the Berkshires, now find inspiration strolling the grounds at Edith Wharton's former grand manse, the Mount. Today, there are many inns, bed and breakfasts, health-conscious retreats and full-service resorts in the surrounding hills.

As you drive down Route 7A into town, a row of massive, old white "cottages" trimmed with wrought-iron hardware welcomes you into the quiet hub. Town center is only a few blocks long with the shop-lined streets, Church and Main, acting as parallel main drags. Along these blocks, art galleries are plentiful as are trendy but low-key cafes and well-dressed

Blantyre ▪ Blueberry pancakes ▪ A Blantyre bedroom ▪ The inn's porch

patrons. An afternoon could be spent wandering from one shop to the next, chatting with the locals.

When you first arrive, you can get your bearings by taking a quick drive southwest of town on Route 183 toward the Stockbridge Bowl (formed by Lake Mahkeenac) and Tanglewood. Drive a loop around the bowl: Take Route 183 until it turns into Interlaken Road, then veer left on Interlaken Cross. Take a left onto Prospect Hill, which turns into Hawthorne. Hawthorne intersects with Route 183, which you can follow back into town. The views from Hawthorne Road are the same ones summer spectators enjoy sitting on the lawn at Tanglewood.

By now, the peaceful streets and long drive may leave you wanting a comfortable bed to tumble into. From the town center, follow Walker Street east, crossing over Route 7. Make your first right onto Blantyre Road to reach your final destination.

POOL AT BLANTYRE

stay

★★★★★ Blantyre

16 Blantyre Road, Lenox, 413-637-3556; www.blantyre.com

The long driveway leading up to this Gilded Age Tudor-style mansion lasts just long enough to melt away any knots you may have gathered during the drive. Built in 1902 to resemble then-owner Robert Paterson's mother's ancestral Scottish home, the ivy-covered structure looks like a small castle both inside and out. Turrets and towers frame the main building, while the carriage house stables and "potting shed" (which now houses the property's spa) are more modern structures. The rooms throughout Blantyre maintain a decidedly British country style, with floral fabrics and overstuffed furniture. You'll find fresh flowers throughout the house arranged courtesy of an in-house florist. The rooms, which are named for their various design themes, like Toile and Crimson, each have their own flavor, some being more feminine and frilly, others feeling grand and luxurious. Fireplaces and soaking tubs are available in many rooms in the main house; a few two-story rooms occupy the carriage house; and the icehouse acts as an individual apartment with a full kitchen and two bedrooms. Guests are known to relax in their own "wings" only to emerge for their dinner reservation. The spa is a short walk from the main property and offers a number of treatments like massages, facials and manicures. A large, bubbling hot tub enclosed in a glass atrium anchors one end of the spa and looks out to the small but tidy swimming pool. There's also a compact workout center but activities like croquet, tennis, swimming and ice skating take place on the vast grounds surrounding the house.

25 rooms. Children over 12 years only. Complimentary continental breakfast. High-speed Internet access. Restaurant, bar. Spa. $$$$

★★★Wheatleigh

Hawthorne Road, Lenox, 413-637-0610; www.wheatleigh.com

An alternative to a stay at Blantyre, this 19th-century Italianate palazzo is set on 22 acres of rolling hills and lush gardens. The interiors present a crisp, contemporary approach to classic sensibilities and highlight the harmony with its natural surroundings. Guest rooms are comfortably elegant with English soaking tubs, exclusive French bath amenities from Ermenegildo Zegna, raw silk coverlets, and CD players. Details make the difference here, from the dazzling Tiffany windows to the ornate fireplace in the Great Hall, along with dark satiny woods and elaborately decorative mantles. Dine on spectacular contemporary French cuisine in a sun-drenched restaurant filled with oil paintings, hand-carved Chippendale chairs and a large wood-burning fireplace.

19 rooms. Children over 9 years only. Wireless Internet access. Two restaurants, bar. Fitness center. Spa. Pool. Tennis. $$$

eat

★★★Blantyre

16 Blantyre Road, Lenox, 413-637-3556;
www.blantyre.com

Dining at this 1902 mansion is a rare culinary experience. Diners enjoy pre-dinner champagne and canapés on the terrace or in the ornately decorated music room before feasting on chef Christopher Brooks' rich, out-of-this-world fare; he fills his dishes with opulent ingredients like foie gras, lobster sauces and creamy chocolates. Antique glassware, place settings and freshly arranged flowers on each table combine to create a romantic atmosphere, and the service is impeccable. Allow Luc Chevalier, the lively and knowledgeable sommelier, to guide you through the 2,300 vintages.

French menu. Breakfast, lunch, dinner. Jacket required. Reservations recommended. Valet parking. $$$

★★★Bistro Zinc

56 Church St., Lenox, 413-637-8800;
www.bistrozinc.com

This lively hotspot is a top choice for locals who fill the tables and eat at the bar well into the night. It's also a good spot for a pre-concert meal. The contemporary décor features black and white herringbone tile, tin ceilings, pale yellow walls, burgundy banquettes and a large copper bar. French-American fusion standouts include duck confit with braised greens and escargots persillade with brioche points. The bar is open until 1 a.m.

French bistro menu. Lunch, dinner, late-night. Bar. Casual attire. Reservations recommended. $$$

WHEATLEIGH

VIEWS FROM THE WHEATLEIGH VERANDA

★★★The Wyndhurst Restaurant
55 Lee Road, Lenox, 413-637-1364; www.cranwell.com
Cranwell Resort's main dining room is on the first floor of the 100-year-old Tudor mansion. Large windows offer vistas of the Berkshire Hills and the fireplace keeps the room warm on cold New England nights. The American cuisine highlights local produce, including game and cheeses.
American. Lunch, dinner. Business casual attire. Reservations recommended. Valet parking. $$$

Wheatleigh's dining room ▪ The elegant lounge ▪ A lobster dish ▪ A Wheatleigh bedroom

see
Berkshire Botanical Garden
Highways 102 and 183, Stockbridge, 413-298-3926;
www.berkshirebotanical.org
This 15-acre botanical garden has perennials, shrubs, trees, antique roses, ponds, a wildflower exhibit, vegetable gardens and demonstration greenhouses. Garden shop; special events, lectures; picnicking. May-October: daily 10 a.m.-5 p.m.

Edith Wharton Estate (The Mount)
2 Plunkett St., Lenox, 413-551-5104; www.edithwharton.org
Edith Wharton's summer estate was planned from a book she co-authored in 1897, *The Decoration of Houses*, and built in 1902. The décor is sparse but opulent. The well-kept terraced lawn and gardens are designed to resemble outdoor rooms with unique architectural details throughout. It's an elegant respite filled with shallow pools and graveled pathways. The enormous Classical Revival house is continuously being restored.
May-October: daily 9 a.m.-4 p.m.

Norman Rockwell Museum
9 Glendale Road, Stockbridge, 413-298-4100; www.nrm.org
The artist's eponymous museum maintains and exhibits the nation's largest collection of original works by Norman Rockwell, who spent a great deal of time capturing the spirit of these very towns. The painter's studio can be seen inside and there's a sculpture by Rockwell's son, Peter, on the lawn. Exhibits rotate throughout the year. Daily 10 a.m.-5 p.m. (except November-April, weekdays 10 a.m.-4 p.m.)

Tanglewood

297 West St., Lenox, 413-637-1600;
www.tanglewood.org

Nathaniel Hawthorne planned *Tanglewood Tales*
here. Many of the 526 acres, developed into a
gentleman's estate by William Aspinwall Tap-
pan, take the form of formal gardens. Well-known
today as the summer home of the Boston Symphony Orchestra, the outdoor music venue stages
concerts—rock, country and classical—all season
long. Seats on the lawn look out beyond the stage
and over Stockbridge Bowl. Go early on nights
when big names are playing to find a spot on the
lawn; stretch out your blanket and bring a picnic
just like the locals do. Visit the Web site for tickets
and pricing.

drive

As tough as it is to tear away from such luxurious
environs, the drive back to Boston will allow for a
few more hours of relaxation. Avoid the Mass Pike
and start south on Route 7 towards Great Barrington; it will lead you through the heart of this
quintessential New England town. A quick stop
to stroll through Railroad Street brings you past
boutiques, galleries and home décor stores. Refuel
for the road at Rubiners.

eat

Rubiners Cheesemongers & Grocers and Rubi's Cafe

264 Main St., Great Barrington, 413-528-0488

This cheese shop, grocer and café carries charcuterie boards and beautiful, hard-to-find cheeses
from around the world. Fresh, overstuffed sandwiches and coffees are available at the café; the
entrance is down the alley. Ask the staff at either to
pack a picnic for your drive back.
Monday-Saturday 10 a.m.-6 p.m., Sunday 10
a.m.-4 p.m.; Rubi's, Monday-Saturday 7:30 a.m.-6
p.m., Sunday 7:30 a.m.-4 p.m. $$

drive

For a longer detour and to stretch your legs, con-
tinue south on Route 7 towards Sheffield. Fields
that are covered in wild flowers in the spring and
summer come into view and a handful of antique
shops and garden centers sit along this road. About
a mile from Sheffield, turn off onto Route 7A and

THE MOUNT

follow signs for Weatogue Road. This will take you to the parking lot and entrance of Bartholomew's Cobble.

see
Bartholomew's Cobble
Ashley Falls, Sheffield, 413-229-8600; www.thetrustees.org
This delicate woodland area is covered with meadows and rocky inlets. There are many easy, interconnecting walking trails which all lead up to Hurlburt's Hill. It provides an incredible view of the Housatonic River Valley. Visitor Center: Daily 9 a.m.-4:30 p.m.

drive
From the Cobble, backtrack over to Route 7 and continue on through Great Barrington, keeping an eye out for signs to Route 23. Follow the hilly, twisting length of this highway past Lake Garfield on your left and then on past the grassy fields of Otis. The road turns at Otis so continue to follow signs, making a left to stay on Route 23. From there, you'll climb up into the woods passing a few handicraft and textile stores. At Woronoco, look for signs leading to Route 20; veer right and follow it into the old industrial township of Westfield. In the middle of town, you'll make a left onto Route 202 which takes you north toward the Mass Pike. From here, we recommend shooting down the long stretch of I-90 to get back to Boston. The final hour should be a peaceful, relaxing stretch taking you the rest of the way home.

CHAPTER 2
DENVER TO ASPEN

It's no surprise that each year, thousands of locals and tourists leave the urbanized metropolis of Denver behind for the splendor of the Colorado Rocky Mountains, a magnificent journey that begins just 20 minutes west of Denver, on Interstate 70, a modern, 450-mile expansive freeway that unleashes some of the most spectacular scenery in Colorado. Here you'll find hushed forests of fir, pine and spruce trees, lush groves of quaking aspens, craggy, 14,000-foot mountain peaks, rippling streams stocked with trout, glistening lakes and scenic highways and byways.

Add unparalleled skiing, a bumper crop of summer outdoor pursuits and quaint mountain towns (their historic avenues flush with convivial restaurants and funky boutiques) to the mix, and you'll understand why weekends are full of warriors heading for the high country.

The drive from Denver to Aspen is especially inspiring, most notably in the fall when the Aspen leaves showcase their chromatic color changes. While the most engaging towns and sites are situated along I-70, Aspen itself is off the beaten path, nesting on its own swatch of beautiful road.

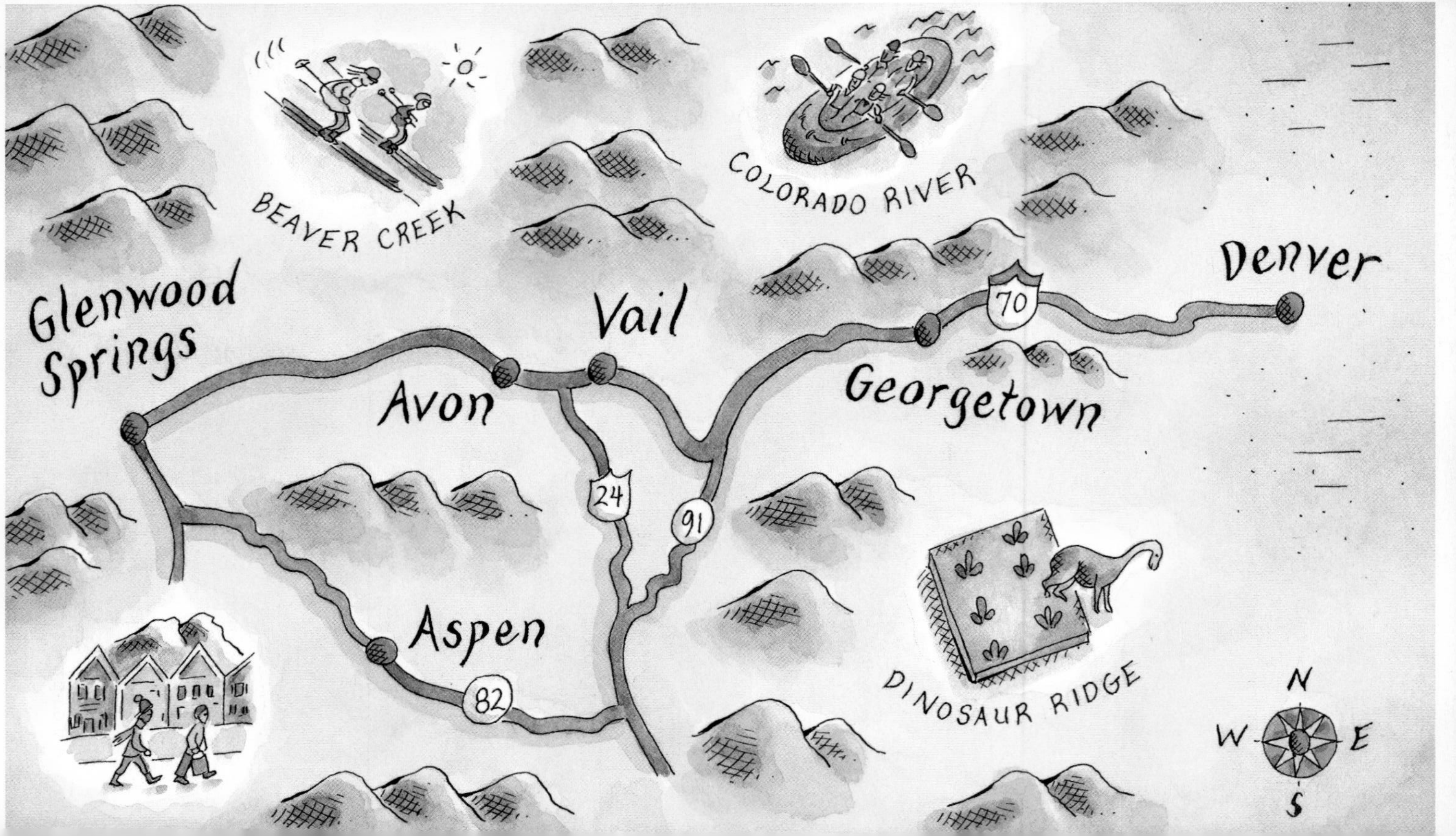

Denver
70
Georgetown
COLORADO RIVER
BEAVER CREEK
Glenwood Springs
Vail
Avon
24
91
Aspen
82
DINOSAUR RIDGE
N
W
E
S

ASPEN

starting out

If you're staying in Denver for a night or two, book a room at the **Brown Palace Hotel** *(321 17th St., Denver, 303-297-3511, 800-321-2599; www. brownpalace.com).* The historic hotel, open since 1892, is an afternoon tea kind of place with luxurious guest rooms in either a Victorian or Art Deco style, and the restaurant is one of Denver's best.

drive

As you journey west out of Denver on I-70 toward Colorado's majestic Rocky Mountains, a myriad of noteworthy attractions could stretch the four-hour drive to Aspen into a three-day weekend, which is what often happens once you start noticing the neck-jerking, jaw-dropping diversions—astounding rock formations, grazing buffalo herds, kaleidoscopic Victorian houses and big horn sheep—that greet you at nearly every bend.

You'll stay on or close to I-70 during the majority of your trip, until you reach Glenwood Springs, a bustling town that paves the way toward the glitzy town of Aspen. The freeway drive is a cinch for locals who head to the mountains at every opportunity, but if you're visiting for the first time, be prepared for the distractions that lie ahead. The scenery alone causes constant head-turning, making it easy to take your eyes of the road. And while I-70 is a major highway with visible signage, road warnings and mile markers, there are precarious downhill voyages, dark tunnels and sharp turns along the way.

Instead of putting the pedal to the metal and making a fast beeline toward Aspen, make the most of your weekend trip by stopping (and gawking) at these vantage points and destinations between Denver and Georgetown, a lovely respite in which to enjoy a late breakfast or lunch.

see
Dinosaur Ridge

16831 W. Alameda Parkway, Morrison, 303-697-3466; www.dinoridge.org
As you crest the first hill that leaves Denver looming in the background, you'll see a sign for Morrison (Exit 259), which leads you to Dinosaur Ridge, a short pilgrimage off the freeway that's worth the detour. This site of di-

nosaur bones, dating back to 1877, is both an outdoor geological site and indoor museum. Free and open year-round for self-guided tours, the easily hikeable one-mile ridge rewards visitors with more than 300 fossilized bones and sandstone-preserved footprints. On various Saturdays and holidays, from May until October, volunteer guides are on hand to answer questions about the fossil remains. Open daily from sunrise to sunset.

Buffalo Herd Outlook
Genesee Park
Back on I-70, heading west, take exit 254 to witness one of Colorado's most talked-about tourist attractions: herds of buffalo grazing in the expansive meadowed pastures. It's not a foregone conclusion that they'll be camera-ready, but more often than not, you can see them lumbering along—and often sleeping. Don't try to feed them, don't chase them and whatever you do, don't play superhero and try to jump the fence that protects their territory. Take photos from a distance.

Sleeper House
South side of I-70, atop Genesee Mountain, at about mile marker 255
Just across the freeway and high on the hilltop of Genesee Mountain sits what is arguably the state's most celebrated slumbering pad. Shaped like a clam, this fascinating sculptured house, encased in glass, played a starring role in Woody Allen's 1973 comedy *Sleeper*—and to this day, locals refer to it as the "Sleeper House."

Starbucks
999 County Road 308, Exit 235, Dumont, 303-567-4530
We're not actually advocating that you stop at Starbucks simply for a jolt of java (although there's really

no inopportune time to grab a latte), but here's a best-kept locals' secret: Directly behind this particular Starbucks, there's a rocky hillside that's one of the best vantage points along I-70 to stand fixated while herds of big horn sheep vie for the right to stand solo at the top of the peak. If you've never seen big horn sheep lock horns in the wild, here's your golden opportunity.

stop
Forty-five miles west of Denver, just off Exit 228, the picturesque village of Georgetown, named for an 1859 silver mining camp, is dotted with historic homes and buildings, their restored Victorian facades tricked out in candied hues. The downtown historic district beckons with its shops, museums and restaurants, while the Georgetown Loop Railroad, a six-mile tour that takes passengers from Georgetown to the nearby town of Silver Plume (and back) via a narrow gauge steam train, is one of the state's most popular side trips.

eat
★Happy Cooker
412 Sixth St., Georgetown, 303-569-3166
This cheekily named spot serves up bountiful breakfasts, soul-satisfying soups, hefty sandwiches on house-baked breads and crepes served in a lovely converted house in Georgetown's historic downtown area.
American menu. Breakfast, lunch. Children's menu. Outdoor seating. $

drive
Once you leave Georgetown en route to Avon/Edwards, a distance of 62 miles, the stretch of I-70 toward Loveland Basin, a ski area just 12 miles west of Georgetown,

and ultimately the 1.7 mile long Eisenhower Tunnel, climbs to an elevation of more than 11,000 feet. The Tunnel, which is the highest vehicular tunnel in the world, journeys through the Continental Divide and lies entirely within the Arapahoe National Forest.

As you exit the Eisenhower Tunnel, the highway descends down a steep hill that takes you into Summit County, a year-round playground for outdoor enthusiasts, offering skiing, boating, windsurfing, fishing, cycling and hiking opportunities amid the area's mountain valleys, steep canyons, sparkling reservoir, and rippling creeks and rivers. You'll whiz by several towns— Dillon, Silverthorne and Frisco—all of which are worth a stop, before the road curves and you pass Copper Mountain, a popular ski resort that sits on the eastern edge of Vail Pass, one of Colorado's highest mountain passes.

With an elevation of 10,666 feet, Vail Pass, steeped in Rocky Mountain splendor and surrounded by forested hillsides, biking trails and towering peaks, makes for a gorgeous drive during the warm months, but during winter snowstorms, it can be one of the most harrowing drives in Colorado. Still, as you cruise down the hill that slopes into the lush valley that's home to the resort town of Vail, you can't help but bask in its unrivaled beauty.

Whitewater rafting on the Colorado River ▪ Frisco ▪ Aspen Mountain in summer ▪ Vail foliage

Once you pass Vail and its neighboring town of Minturn, a groovy, laid-back hamlet steeped in history, the scenery becomes decidedly more arid, with small bushes and brush on the northern side of the highway. On the south side of the highway, however, the mountains tilt skyward, their crests looming in the distance. Stay the night in Avon, at the Ritz-Carlton Bachelor Gulch, but before you get there, take the time to stop at some of these destinations between Georgetown and Avon.

see
SILVERTHORNE
146-V Rainbow Drive, 970-746-7686; www.outletsatsilverthorne.com
Dating back to the 1860s, this bustling town, off Exit 205, is a popular tourist stop for shopping, thanks to the 70 factory outlet stores just off the highway. Stock up on ski or outdoor wear at Columbia Sportswear, Eddie Bauer or Timberland. You'll also find a slew of stores like Coach, Tommy Hilfiger, Polo, Harry & David and Calvin Klein.

BIKING IN VAIL

FRISCO
120 Main St., 970-668-3428; www.townoffrisco.com
Just west of Silverthorne, in the center of Summit County, this picturesque village, framed by skyscraping peaks, trumpets a charming downtown area abundant with antiquated wooden cabins, excellent restaurants and watering holes, boutiques and galleries. But the best reason to stop here is to tour Frisco Historic Park, a collection of seven buildings dating back to the late 19th century. Meander through the one-room schoolhouse, chapel, mining center and jail and then head inside to the museum to peruse the fascinating artifacts reflecting the town's rich history.

VAIL
Exit 176, 877-204-7881; www.visitvailvalley.com, www.vail.snow.com
The European-inspired village of Vail—in the Gore Creek Valley, between the Gore and Sawatch mountain ranges, about 100 miles west of Denver and 20 minutes east of Avon—has garnered a sterling worldwide reputation for its rustic cobblestone streets, elegant architecture and unparalleled skiing. You could easily spend a day (or more) here window-shopping, restaurant-hopping and exploring both the Colorado Ski Museum and Betty Ford Alpine Gardens, which sprout roughly 2,000 species of plants, plus a 120-foot waterfall, Asian meditation garden and picnic areas. At 8,200 feet, it's the highest alpine botanical garden in North America.

stop
Twenty minutes west of Vail and just a few minutes down the valley from Beaver Creek Resort, in the bedroom communities of Avon and Edwards, locals lounge on the expansive patios of trendy restaurants and bars, shop like big city diehards, and fly by on their mountain bikes, a testament to the serious outdoor pursuits that make these burgeoning mountain burgs bona fide recreational paradises. A decade ago, Avon and Edwards—both of which enjoy the benefit of banking on the Eagle River— barely boasted more than a gas station and a lone restaurant. Today, the towns still maintain their easygoing vibe, but a cornucopia of chic boutiques, hip cafés and friendly bars has added an infectious energy that rivals their glitzy ski resort neighbors.

RITZ-CARLTON BACHELOR GULCH

stay

★★★★Ritz-Carlton Bachelor Gulch
0130 Daybreak Ridge, Avon, 970-748-6200; www.ritzcarlton.com
Rugged meets refined at this ski-in/ski-out resort, located at the base of the mountain at Beaver Creek. From Bachelor, (the lovable Golden Retriever that greets you upon check-in) to the stunningly appointed Spago restaurant, this high-altitude resort captures the spirit of the Old West while incorporating understated elegance and opulence. The spacious rooms and suites, bedecked with leather chairs, dark wood furniture and wood-beamed ceilings, are comfortable and stylish. Iron chandeliers, fireplaces and twig furnishings adorn the public spaces. This family-friendly resort also offers an abundance of activities, including fly fishing, a horseshoe pit, two children's play areas, an outdoor pool, spa services, golf and skiing right outside your back door.
180 rooms. Wireless Internet access. Two restaurants, bar. Spa. Ski-in/ski-out. Golf. Tennis. Business center. Pets accepted. $$$$

eat

★★★Grouse Mountain Grill
141 Scott Hill Road, Avon, 970-949-0600; www.grousemountaingrill.com
Located in the Pines Lodge, this elegant, European-style restaurant is the perfect choice for breakfast, lunch or a quiet dinner. The dark wood furnishings, nightly piano music and tables topped with crisp white linens create a warm and cozy atmosphere. The dinner menu focuses on rustic American dishes such as grilled Yukon River salmon with crab bread pudding and cracked mustard sauce, and pretzel-crusted pork chops with orange mustard sauce and balsamic syrup. The warm apple bread pudding is a sweet finale.
American menu. Dinner. Closed mid-April to mid-May. Bar. Casual attire. Valet parking. Outdoor seating. $$$

PEAK SEASON

In early 2008, the town of Avon introduced the Riverfront Express Gondola, which provides the fastest route from Avon to Beaver Creek Mountain. The three-minute gondola ride whisks skiers and snowboarders to Beaver Creek Landing, where two existing, high-speed chairlifts deliver guests to the main ski mountain. By the end of 2008, Avon will unveil the Westin Riverfront Resort and Spa as part of the town's much anticipated Riverfront Village. In addition to the new Westin, the Village will also boast a river front park, restaurants, shops, bike paths and bars.

EDWARDS

Eat! Drink!
56 Edwards Village Blvd., Edwards, 970-926-1393; www.eatdrinkinc.com
An artisanal cheesier, panini and small plates palace, gourmet food
emporium and fancified wine boutique all rolled into one, this bright,
contemporary-styled gathering place is a terrific spot for lunch or an early
dinner. You can nosh on everything from olive boats and antipasto plates to
pressed sandwiches and flatbread dotted with creamy burrata and tarped
with prosciutto.
Italian menu. Lunch, dinner. $$

Larkburger
Edwards Village Center
105 Edwards Village Blvd., Edwards, 970-926-9336; www.larkburger.com
There are your run-of-the-mill burger barns—and then there is Larkburger,
a gourmet burger haven that slides its organic meat patties onto all-natural
buns sided with the requisite accompaniments: in-season tomatoes, leafy
lettuce, the joint's secret house-made sauce, and a litany of adornments,
including Tillamook cheddar and truffle aïoli. The burgers are wrapped in
wax paper and arrive à la carte, which means that the hand-cut truffle and
Parmesan-dusted French fries are an extra indulgence.
Burger menu. Lunch, dinner. $

Route 6 Café
41310 US Highway 6, Avon, 970-949-6393
If you want to have breakfast with the locals, it's worth braving the waits
at this packed-to-the-rafters food temple, a renovated gas station that
parades the Vail Valley's best eggs Benedict, corned beef hash and pan-
cakes in a kitschy dining room bolstered by friendly servers and top-drawer
bloody marys.
American menu. Breakfast. $

Spago
0130 Daybreak Ridge, Avon, 970-343-1555; www.ritzcarlton.com
The Spago team—Wolfgang Puck, executive chef Mark Ferguson and
renowned New York-based interior designer Tony Chi—have created a
spectacular-looking restaurant located in the Ritz that's a head-turning

combination of modern Manhattan chic and rustic Rocky Mountain elegance. The contemporary, seasonally inspired menu encompasses swoonworthy dishes that hopscotch from handmade pumpkin agnolotti and ricotta gnocchi with lamb Bolognese to splendid breakfast offerings like the corned beef hash, eggs Benedict and truffled parmesan polenta crowned with yolky organic eggs.

Contemporary American cuisine. Breakfast, lunch, dinner. Casual attire. Bar. Reservations recommended. $$$$

Vin 48 Restaurant & Wine Bar

48 E. Beaver Creek Blvd., Avon, 970-748-9463; www.vin48.com

The 32-foot ceilings and huge windows are reason enough to visit this contemporary American food temple, which parades small plates like the mussels bobbing in a roasted green curry sauce and large plates such as the pan-roasted wild striped bass sided with tiger shrimp ravioli. Sit at the chefs' counter and watch the seamless kitchen work its magic as you sip from the map-spanning wine roster that also happens to offer more than 40 pours by the glass, both in three- and six-ounce servings. American menu. Dinner $$

SUMMER IN ASPEN

spa

★★★★Bachelor Gulch Spa at the Ritz-Carlton

0130 Daybreak Ridge, Avon, 970-748-6200; www.ritzcarlton.com

The Bachelor Gulch Spa captures the essence of its alpine surroundings with polished rock, stout wood and flowing water in its interiors. The rock grotto with a lazy river hot tub is a defining feature, and the fitness rooms have majestic mountain views. The beauty of the outdoors also extends to treatments that utilize ingredients indigenous to the region. Alpine berries, Douglas fir and blue spruce sap are just some of the natural components of the exceptional signature treatments. After a rigorous day on the slopes, there are also plenty of massage options, from the Roaring Rapids, which uses hydrotherapy, or the Four-Hands, where two therapists work out knots.

WINTER IN ASPEN

see

Beaver Creek/Arrowhead Resort
137 Benchmark Road, Avon, 970-949-5750; www.beavercreek.com
Ten quad, two triple, three double chairlifts, oh my! This deluxe outdoor playground guarantees total skier satisfaction with everything from rental equipment and snowmaking capabilities to nearly 3-mile-long runs and a vertical drop of 4,040 feet. Those with less of an affinity for double black diamonds can treat themselves to ice skating, snowmobiling and sleigh rides. Chairlift rides are a fun way to see the mountain in the warmer months.

Colorado River Runs
Rancho del Rio, 28 miles northwest off Highway 131, 800-826-1081, 970-653-4292; www.coloradoriverruns.com
Raft down the Colorado River. Tours depart from Rancho del Rio (just outside State Bridge) and last two-and-a-half to three hours.

Eagle Valley Trail
Join the trail at Highway 6 and Spur Road directly behind the Riverwalk at Edwards
Lace up your walking shoes and meander along the scenic Eagle Valley trail, a winding paved path that follows the roaring Eagle River before crossing the bridge to Freedom Park, a forested area in which to picnic, play volleyball and practice your latest skateboarding pivots.

drive

It's a 93-mile drive from Avon to Aspen, half of which is spent on I-70, while the final half of the drive journeys along CO-82 through the towns of Glenwood Springs, Basalt and El Jebel. As you leave Avon, heading west toward Glenwood Springs, the Rockies' rugged peaks intersect with small hamlets, many of them burgeoning with new housing communities and commerce.

The highway is steep and twisting before it ventures into the crevices of Glenwood Canyon, a 12-mile stretch of roadway bordered by steep canyon walls carved by the Colorado River, which flows below. Without question, this is one of the most dramatic stretches of highway in Colorado. As the canyon begins to widen, you'll see the turn-off (Exit 116) for Glenwood Springs on your right. This picturesque town, encased by the White River National Forest, sports a rugged landscape blanketed with mountain trails, forested hillsides and skyscraping peaks, all of which you'll see as you drive on CO-82 toward your final destination of Aspen, though we recommend stopping and having a look around. The town is known for its behemoth hot springs pool, a mineral-laden steam haven in the winter and sun-kissed splashing ground in the summer. The **Glenwood Caverns and Historic Fairy Caves** (*51000 Two Rivers Plaza Road, Glenwood Springs, 970-945-4228; www.glenwoodcaverns.com*), just recently opened to the public after lying dormant since 1917, and are a fascinating foray into the world of underground labyrinths.

stop

Welcome to Aspen, Colorado's most prestigious playground for snow bunnies, A-list celebrities and affluent jetsetters. Originally a mining town, Aspen is now an enchanting paradise touting swanky hotels, excellent restaurants, cultural attractions and four separate ski areas, including world-renowned Aspen Mountain. Stay at least a night to explore the town's many riches.

THE ST. REGIS

stay

★★★★★The Little Nell

675 E. Durant Ave., Aspen, 970-920-4600; www.thelittlenell.com

A ski-in/ski-out property nesting at the base of Aspen Mountain, the Little Nell covets an ideal location for schussing down the slopes or roaming the streets of Aspen in search of some of the state's best boutiques and restaurants. The rooms and suites are heavenly cocoons with fireplaces, overstuffed furniture and luxurious bathrooms. Some suites feature vaulted ceilings showcasing glorious mountainside views, while others overlook the buzzing streets. Enjoy the well-equipped fitness center and outdoor pool and Jacuzzi. Montagna restaurant is one of the most popular dining destinations in town, thanks to its inventive reinterpretation of American cuisine, while the Torrace Bar at the Little Nell is a see-and-be-seen spot for après ski.

92 rooms. Closed late April to mid-May. High-speed Internet access. Ski-in/ski-out. Three restaurants, two bars. Airport transportation available. Pool. Business center. Pets accepted. $$$$

★★★★The St. Regis Aspen

315 E. Dean St., Aspen, 970-920-3300, 888-454-9005;
www.stregis.com/aspen

Just steps away from Aspen Mountain, between the gondola and lift, this hotel's upscale Western atmosphere is the perfect respite from a day of powder-pushing, power-shopping and warm weather activities such as fly-fishing and whitewater rafting. The outdoor pool and accompanying lounge are ideal for whiling away warm afternoons, or you can relax in the lavish spa. Rooms are richly decorated with bursts of color and oversized leather furniture (expect complimentary water bottle service and a humidifier at turndown). The Club Floor offers its own concierge and five complimentary meals throughout the day. Olives Aspen serves Mediterranean-inspired cuisine from renowned chef Todd English, and Whiskey Rocks is a popular place to mingle.

253 rooms. Closed late October to mid-November. High-speed Internet access. Restaurant, two bars. Airport transportation available. $$$$

Aspen Moutain • The Little Nell • Views from the St. Regis • The Little Nell

eat

★★★★Montagna

675 E. Durant Ave., Aspen, 970-920-4600; www.thelittlenell.com

With its butter-hued walls, tapestry carpets, iron chandeliers and deep picture windows, Montagna, the signature restaurant in The Little Nell hotel, resonates with Old World warmth and intimacy. The seasonally inspired menu, which includes ingredients from chef Ryan Hardy's own farm, parades indelible Rocky Mountain Artisan cuisine (think pan-roasted black cod, roasted pork tenderloin with braised bacon and butternut squash ravioli), a perfect foil for master sommelier Richard Betts' 15,000-bottle private wine cellar.

American menu. Breakfast, lunch, dinner, Sunday brunch. Closed late April to mid-May. Bar. Children's menu. Casual attire. Valet parking. Outdoor seating. $$$$

★★★Olives

315 E. Dean St., Aspen, 970-920-3300; www.toddenglish.com

Olives, located in the St. Regis, delivers American cuisine with strong Mediterranean influences. The seasonal menu incorporates local ingredients and features favorites like skillet-seared Rocky Mountain trout, truffle-smoked pheasant ravioli and paella risotto. The cozy, dim-lit dining room, bedecked with wrought iron sconces, pinewood floors, antique furniture and a Tuscan-influenced exhibition kitchen, strikes just the right chord.

Mediterranean menu. Lunch, dinner. Children's menu. $$$

★★★Piñons

105 S. Mill St., Aspen, 970-920-2021; www.pinons.net

One of the most sought-after reservations in Aspen, Piñons evokes a casual yet decidedly sophisticated vibe. The intimate dining room, swathed in suede, leather and lodgepole and flanked by a wall of windows, is perpetually packed with locals and out-of-towners who nosh from the New American menu highlighting locally sourced ingredients. Don't miss the foie gras with poached pears and almond brioche, the lobster strudel or the signature New Zealand elk loin, crowned with huckleberry jam and paired with Boursin potatoes and haricot verts.

American menu. Dinner. Closed early April-early June, October-November. Bar. Casual attire. $$$

★★★Syzygy

520 E. Hyman Ave., Aspen, 970-925-3700; www.syzygyrestaurant.com
You might spot a celebrity or two dining at this romantic hot spot that turns out modern American cuisine. Signature dishes include elk tenderloin and vintage beef. The dining room boasts spectacular views of Aspen Mountain, while the jazz room in the back features eight intimate booths.

American menu. Dinner. Closed mid-April to May. Bar. Children's menu. Casual attire. $$$

see

Aspen Mountain

601 E. Dean St., Aspen, 970-925-1220, 800-525-6200; www.aspensnowmass.com/aspen-mountain
Aspen Mountain is a must-ski for any serious downhill enthusiast. A plethora of chairlifts and gondolas, combined with 77 well-groomed runs, the mountain never feels cramped and lift lines move quickly. Ski-schools are led by top notch instructors and shuttle buses provide access to Buttermilk, Aspen Highlands and Snowmass resorts as well.

Blazing Adventures

407 E. Hyman Ave., Aspen, 970-923-4544, 800-282-7238; www.blazingadventures.com
Sign up for some river rafting on the Arkansas, Roaring Fork, Colorado and Gunnison rivers. Trips range from scenic floats for beginners to exciting runs for experienced rafters. Whitewater rafting. Half-day, full-day and overnight. May-October; reservations required. Transportation to site. Bicycle, jeep and hiking tours are also available.

drive

While the easiest way back to Denver is via I-70, the shortest—and most scenic route—is on Highway 82 over Independence Pass. It's a spectacular visual treat, not to mention an adrenaline rush, although if heights, hairpin turns and narrow roads make your heart palpitate, you may want to stick to postcards. The 44-mile winding road between Highway 24 and Aspen is among the nation's highest, reaching 12,095 feet at its rocky summit—and offers beautiful vistas of Colorado's majestic forests and peaks at every twist and turn. The best time to visit is during the fall season, when the shimmering aspen trees go from green to golden to crimson. There are numerous hiking trails along the way and the views from the summit are simply spectacular. Take note, however, that the pass is closed between November and May.

Once you descend the pass, you'll follow Highway 91 north past Leadville, another charming mining town, until you pass Copper Mountain, which then takes you to Interstate 70 East—the fast track back to Denver. If you're not in a hurry, we recommend a couple more unique spots you may have missed on your way to Aspen.

see

Idaho Springs

Exit 241-A; www.idahospringsco.com
The former site of a major gold strike in 1859, this charming Victorian town, 35 miles west of Denver, is worth a stop, if for no other reason

ASPEN

than to view Bridal Veil Falls plunging through the largest historic water wheel in Colorado.

Ski Country Antiques
114 Homestead Road, Evergreen, 303-674-4666; www.skicountryantiques.com
This 20,000-square-foot antiques emporium peddles more than 15,000 pieces, many of which celebrate the state's obsession with outdoor sports and recreation. You'll encounter everything from antique skis and military snowshoes to canoes and toboggans. The behemoth warehouse also features a slew of European antiques, vintage photos, antler chandeliers and log cabin furnishings.

CHAPTER 3
LOS ANGELES TO LA JOLLA

In the movies people may ride off into the sunset, but in and around L.A., the streets and highways are filled with lanes of cars slowly inching forward. For many, Southern California conjures up movie stars, palm trees...and traffic. But once you're out of the gridlock, it's a different picture. Southern California is blessed with stunning coastline, snow-topped mountains, rich fertile valleys and a Joshua tree-studded desert, all of which is best seen from behind the wheel.

One of the best ways to experience Southern California's beauty is to take the two-and-a-half hour coastal drive from Los Angeles to La Jolla, and explore everything in between. There is much to see and do, and we've selected the best places to stop, stay and eat. Why La Jolla? The final destination is one of the most luxurious properties anywhere: The Lodge at Torrey Pines. It's definitely worth a visit and is the perfect place to end up after hours on the road. So, charge your iPod, put on your sleekest shades and get ready for the ride.

starting out

The **Peninsula Beverly Hills** (*9882 S. Santa Monica Blvd., Beverly Hills, 310-551-2888; www.beverlyhills.peninsula.com*) is a good choice while in L.A. The Five-Star French Renaissance-style hotel has oversized marble tubs, state-of-the-art electronic systems and meticulous gardens.

drive

Congestion in L.A. can occur at any time. Your best bet is to avoid rush hours and listen to local radio for updates on jams before you approach them. (Tune in on KNX AM 1070 or KFI AM 640 for these reports.) In any case, you're on a road trip, so try to enjoy your time on *the road*.

PENINSULA BEVERLY HILLS

For those who have a need for speed, the trip is simple: take Interstate 5 all the way to sunny San Diego. Otherwise, opt for the much more scenic route down Highway 1 (popularly known as the Pacific Coast Highway or PCH) south until you reach Dana Point in south Orange County, where it ends. The trip on PCH will add hours to the drive, but will also treat you to some of the most breathtaking vistas in the country.

If you are leaving from the Hollywood area, take the 101 south until you hit Interstate 5. Also known as the Golden State Freeway, I-5 stretches from the U.S.-Mexican border through Oregon and is the main artery that connects Los Angeles, Orange and San Diego counties. From I-5, merge onto Interstate 10 (also known as the Santa Monica Freeway) and head west until you hit the Pacific Ocean, and Highway 1. If you are leaving from West Los Angeles (Westwood, Santa Monica or West Hollywood) neighborhoods, take the 405 freeway south to the 10 freeway west.

Once you've finagled your way onto Highway 1, the trip is a breeze—an ocean breeze that is, with the water and cream-colored beach to your right and sandy cliffs to your left. If you're heading out early in the day and want to stop for breakfast, take a two-mile detour north on Highway 1 (at the Entrada exit) for a worthwhile stop at Patrick's Roadhouse.

SAILBOATS IN NEWPORT BEACH

eat

Patrick's Roadhouse

106 Entrada Drive, Los Angeles, 310-459-4544; www.patricksroadhouse.info
You'll spot this humble but charming breakfast joint just west of L.A.'s
downtown by its bright green exterior and shamrock motif. Sounds kitschy,
but its cover does not define the goods inside. Look for a seat toward the
back where you'll find historical accounts of California through framed clips
of old magazine articles and turn-of-the-century oil paintings, or at the front
where the ocean breeze comes straight at you through the open windows
and doors. Patrick's serves breakfast staples including a dozen different
omelets as well as burgers and sandwiches for lunch, amidst a mellow,
pleasant ambience.
American menu. Breakfast, lunch. $

drive

After you've had your fill, return to Highway 1 and head south. If you opt
to stick with the longer drive via this route, take note that the entire drive is
not scenic. It does, however, cut through all of southern California's best
beaches, including Santa Monica beach, Venice beach and Redondo and
Manhattan beaches in the South Bay region of Los Angeles. But before you
get to Orange County's beaches, Highway 1 zigzags through LAX International Airport and Long Beach and Seal Beach, where much of the drive is
considerably distant from the ocean. The route becomes more scenic and
picturesque along Huntington State Beach, where the sand stretches for
miles. This is a particularly handsome drive, especially during sunset when
the sinking sun blazes orange light on the sandy beaches lined with tall
palm trees. The ocean lies right next to your car once you get to the Huntington Beach Pier, then spreads away as you see more of the pale sand
stretch toward the water. If you're thirsty, Huntington Beach's Main Street is
filled with bars, restaurants and surf shops for those looking to stretch their
legs. Continue down the coast on Highway 1 toward Newport Beach.

stop

Made famous by recent television dramas and reality TV shows, the communities of Costa Mesa, Newport Beach, Laguna Beach and Dana Point can all be found in southern Orange County. Here, you'll also find some of southern California's most elegant beach resorts, high-end restaurants and beautiful beaches.

Cut through the city of Costa Mesa and you'll suddenly hit a beach city that is distinctive from those up north. Orange County's beaches are noticeably cleaner and in some areas, show off waters as turquoise as those in the Caribbean. Your first stop will be Newport Beach, known for its sandy shores and clear blue waters. Incorporated in 1906 and reigning as one of Orange County's wealthiest neighborhoods, Newport Beach is all about elegance and shopping, yachts with white sails and million dollar properties.

Guest room at the Fairmont Newport Beach ▪ Balboa Pier ▪ The Island Hotel Patio ▪ Fairmont Newport Beach pool

stay

★★★★The Island Hotel, Newport Beach

690 Newport Center Drive, Newport Beach, 866-554-4620;
www.theislandhotel.com

This 20-story tower is angled toward the Pacific Ocean and is only minutes from the beach. Guest rooms are spacious and comfortable with marble bathrooms, luxurious Italian linens and well-appointed workspaces. The private balconies in some suites and furnished patios offer exceptional views of the Pacific Ocean and Newport Harbor. You may never want to leave the pool with its lush landscaping, 17-foot fireplace for chilly evenings and dataports and telephone jacks to stay in touch. Overlooking the nearby islands of Balboa, Lido and Catalina, this Newport Beach gem is only minutes from upscale shopping and golf facilities.

295 rooms. High-speed Internet access. Two restaurants, bar. Fitness center. Spa. Airport transportation available. Business center. Pets accepted. $$$

★★★Fairmont Newport Beach

4500 MacArthur Blvd., Newport Beach, 949-476-2001;
www.fairmont.com/newportbeach

This hotel's most striking feature is its exterior, resembling a modern version of a Mayan temple with its stacked semi-pyramid design. While an

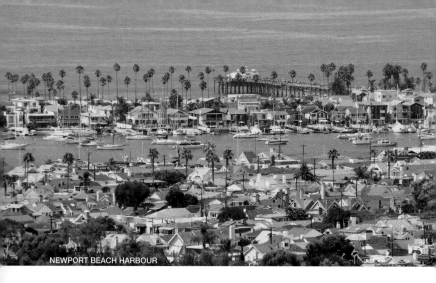
NEWPORT BEACH HARBOUR

ocean view doesn't come with the room rate here (the ocean is about eight miles away from the hotel), don't let this sway any plans to stay. The hotel recently completed a $32 million renovation and the result is a new high-end spa, a redesigned sky pool and luxurious new rooms with Egyptian cotton sheets and flat-screen TVs. And be sure to visit the pool, located next to the spa on the hotel's third floor, where the cabanas are sheathed in golden curtains the color of egg yolks.

440 rooms. High-speed Internet access. Restaurant, bar. Fitness center. Pool. Tennis. Airport transportation available. Spa. Business center. Pets accepted. $$

eat
★★★The Ritz

880 Newport Center Drive, Newport Beach, 949-720-1800;
www.ritzrestaurant.com

The moment you step inside this epicurean eatery, you'll feel transported. Dim lighting is not a bother but a fine comfort; its mellow but rich light is ideal for a romantic dinner or drink. The restaurant's ambience achieves European charm through its dark wood walls, black leather booths and giant bottles of Moët & Chandon champagne that stand behind one particular booth. Yellow chandeliers with light bulbs shaped as bunches of grapes contribute to the golden lighting while potted palms add to the elegance and no fewer than six distinctive, richly appointed indoor and outdoor dining spaces grace the premises. The Escoffier Room (a pavilion-style space that exudes rosy light and with Georgian accents and portraits of the renowned Paris Ritz Hotel chef Auguste Escoffier) is in contrast to the darker, more subdued and private Wine Cellar (a vaulted brick chamber accessed through an oval tunnel that seats large parties of up to 32 people) and the outstanding cuisine encompasses French, Italian and American styles. For lunch, try the wild mushroom "cappuccino," along with the enormous Ritz salad, and leave room for the Harlequin soufflé, made with Belgian chocolate and Grand Marnier served with a Marnier crème anglaise sauce.

American, French menu. Lunch, dinner. Bar. Valet parking. $$$

Mariposa

Neiman Marcus, 601 Newport Center Drive, Newport Beach, 949-467-3350

A day of shopping at Fashion Island is a must, as is lunch afterward at this famed restaurant located on the third floor of Neiman Marcus with views of the mall or the ocean. It may be a casual department store eatery, but the crisp popovers straight out of the oven with strawberry butter and the lobster club hit the spot after power shopping.

American menu. Lunch. $$

Five Crowns

3801 E. Coast Highway, Corona Del Mar, 949-760-0331; www.lawrysonline.com/fivecrowns_gen_info.asp

THE ISLAND HOTEL
POOL AND SPA

The Five Crowns follows the fine tradition of Lawry's The Prime Rib restaurants but remains an original outpost by keeping in the English tradition (made convincing by the red telephone booth outside its entrance). Dark, lush ivy blankets the restaurant's exterior and adds to the old English inn style found here. In addition to juicy cuts of prime rib, you'll find porterhouse steaks, rotisserie free-range chicken and fresh lobster tails.

Steak menu. Dinner, Sunday brunch. Reservations recommended. Valet parking. $$$

spa

★★★★The Spa at the Island Hotel

690 Newport Center Drive, Newport Beach, 949-759-0808, 866-554-4620; www.theislandhotel.com

Slip away to the Spa at the Island Hotel for a muscle-relieving massage or detoxifying volcanic clay treatment that is said to reenergize the body from head to toe. Spacious and modern, the spa's elegant touches—granite floors, silver tea pitchers and a calming water wall—instantly set a tranquil and tasteful tone. The spa's signature rituals use elements from India, Bali and the Hawaiian Islands. The Island Tropical Splendor, for instance, is a full-body scrub blending fresh coconut, rice and vetiver—a perennial grass native to India known for its medicinal and aromatic properties.

see
Balboa Island

Driving north on Highway 1 from Laguna Beach, you'll pass by Balboa Island, a small harbor dotted

FIVE CROWNS RESTAURANT

with yachts and properties perched on the island. Continue driving for about five miles and you'll have access to Newport's gorgeous state beaches. Two favorites among Newport locals include Corona Del Mar and Crystal Cove State Beaches. Newport is also home to one of Orange County's most daring surfing breaks called "the Wedge," located on the southern tip of Balboa Peninsula off Newport where the waves can swell well over 10 feet.

Corona Del Mar

Newport Beach's stretch of Highway 1 is packed with restaurants, bars and boutiques, and also leads to one of the locals' favorite beaches, Corona Del Mar. To get there, continue on Highway 1, southeast from Newport Beach, until you see Marguerite Street, where you will make a right turn.

Crystal Cove State Beach

www.crystalcovestatepark.com/ beaches.htm

As you drive farther south, Newport's landscape will spread out to open hills and an expanse of ocean. Crystal Cove State Beach attracts beach-goers who are looking for a more secluded area and is one of the loveliest beaches you'll see. You can access Crystal Cove beach from Highway 1 and parking costs $10 per day.

Fashion Island

Though Newport is well known as a beach town, it also has some serious shopping centers. Stop by Fashion Island for a shopping fix at Neiman Marcus or Bloomingdale's. The shopping center, encircled by Newport Center Drive, also has hotel accommodations if you can't fit all the retail therapy into one day.

drive

With sand in your shoes and a nice golden glow, hop back in the car and continue south on Highway 1. As you approach Dana Point, you will be forced to merge back onto I-5 as Highway 1 ends here. Luckily, I-5 seems to take over where Highway 1 leaves off, as it hugs the coast for the good portion of the trip to San Diego. A few miles after rejoining I-5, you'll see signs for **San Onofre State Beach** (*Route 5, south of San Clemente, 949-492-4872; www. parks.ca.gov*), which is worth the visit for a quick pit stop and a photo op. You're now halfway between the greater Los Angeles area and San Diego County. You'll know you're passing through San Onofre when you look around and see that there are no homes, buildings or freeway signs, and very few freeway exits. Because the nature area is protected, you'll just see a whole lot of rolling hills, making this a particularly scenic strip of the drive.

Next, you'll pass through Camp Pendleton Marine Corps Base, a 200-square-mile-wide expanse of natural terrain where only electricity poles and a brief view of the ocean are there to keep you company. You will notice very soon, however, two large nuclear plant structures that amount to the San Onofre Nuclear Generating Station, which provides almost 20 percent of the power used by 15 million southern Californians. The area surrounding the plant is one of the most calming parts of the drive, free of traffic jams and junctions. Some stretches still show bits of the ocean, but much of it is solely the landscape of California's dry chaparral hills.

Soon enough, the wide natural expanse will disappear and again, and you'll see the buildings and

CORONA DEL MAR BEACH

congestion of urban California. You are now approaching San Diego's north county. At this point you're still driving well inland of the coast as you pass through the North County coastal communities of Oceanside, Carlsbad, Leucadia, Encinitas, Solana Beach and Del Mar. At last, find yourself in San Diego.

Just before reaching the quiet neighborhood of Encinitas, a new coastal highway opens up: Highway 101. Looking very much like Highway 1, Highway 101 runs briefly along San Diego's north county through Encinitas and ending in Solana Beach. Exit Encinitas Blvd., which will take you to Highway 101 and head south. Here, you'll pass through the small neighborhood of Cardiff by the Sea, home to one of North County's most popular Mexican restaurants. You're now in San Diego territory, where its proximity to the border ensures some authentic Mexican grub.

eat

Las Olas

2655 S. Highway 101, Cardiff by the Sea, 760-942-1860;
www.lasolasmex.com

If you're feeling hunger pangs during this part of the drive, look no further than Las Olas. Named for the waves its location faces, Las Olas (Spanish for "the waves") is known to dish up the best Mexican food in town. Order some fish tacos and enjoy the views. The place also serves fresh, local lobster during the high season between October and March.

Mexican menu. Lunch, dinner. Bar. Children's menu. Casual attire. $

drive

Continuing onward, the coastal highway ekes out as it hits the small community of Del Mar, where the highway becomes Camino Del Mar, which cuts through the coastal edge of the city. As you drive along Camino Del Mar and pass Del Mar Heights, the road will drop steadily downhill as you approach La Jolla. Be sure to go through **Torrey Pines State Reserve**, which abuts the water between Del Mar and La Jolla. Here, you'll encounter a magnificent view of the ocean below, where it faces the Soledad Lagoon. Beyond the beach, you'll see the cascading cliffs of La Jolla

TORREY PINES

covered with a veil of the sea's mist. It's a favorite spot to drive in San Diego for it provides a marvelous transition into La Jolla, the city that sits prettily between North County and south San Diego toward downtown. This is an excellent stop to take a few pictures or breathe in the misty, salty air. Parking is available so pull over, kick off your shoes and sink your feet in the cool sand.

Camino Del Mar turns into North Torrey Pines Road after you pass the Soledad Lagoon. Drive up the hill and enjoy the view of the lagoon for a second time through glimpses in your rearview mirror.

stop

Said to be named for the word "jewel" in Spanish, the small, affluent oceanside neighborhood of La Jolla is home to the University of California, San Diego, the legendary Salk Institute, the Birch Aquarium and the renowned Torrey Pines Golf Course. But the crown jewel here is certainly downtown La Jolla, bordering the town's expansive beach. North Torrey Pines Road will take you downtown by way of winding roads and a slow, downhill approach of the beach. To get there, take La Jolla Shores Drive and turn on Camino del Oro. Downtown La Jolla's best street to browse is Girard Avenue, where there are high-end boutiques, including Ralph Lauren. Park anywhere you can find a spot and begin walking. This portion of La Jolla is packed with art galleries, restaurants and hotels. On Girard, you'll spot a small passage with the sign "Arcade Building," which mimics Parisian-style passage shopping. From Girard, you can walk to La Jolla Cove, where the avenue grows narrow and winds slightly downhill until you see an expanse of sapphire-blue ocean and a large, brightly manicured lawn. Grab a coffee from one of La Jolla's cafés and head down to the sea.

From La Jolla, it's also easy to pop back and forth to San Diego, where you can spend the day touring the Gaslamp Quarter or Balboa Park (the largest urban cultural park in the country boasting an impressive 15 museums, numerous art galleries, free outdoor concerts, the Globe Theatres and a world-famous zoo) or taking in the dining and nightlife. There's never a dull—or cloudy—moment in San Diego. Almost every day is sunny and 70 degrees. (From I-5, exit Front Street to get to the heart of downtown, which runs mostly on one-way streets.)

The Lodge at Torrey Pines (far left, left) • Laurel restaurant (right, far right)

stay

★★★★The Lodge at Torrey Pines
11480 N. Torrey Pines Road, La Jolla, 858-453-4420;
www.lodgetorreypines.com
The Lodge sits on a rocky cliff overlooking the Pacific Ocean and is surrounded by protected forest and unspoiled beaches. The view is gorgeous, but many are drawn by another aspect of the location: the lodge neighbors the 18th hole of the Torrey Pines Golf Course, one of the most acclaimed courses in the world. Tee times are guaranteed for guests who want to try their hand at the championship course. The resort itself is a celebration of the American Craftsman period, from its stained glass and handcrafted woodwork to its Stickley-style furnishings. The warm guest rooms boast custom-designed furniture, modern amenities and spectacular views of the golf course or courtyard.
171 rooms. High-speed Internet access. Two restaurants, two bars. Fitness center. Spa. Tennis. Airport transportation available. $$$

eat

★★★★A.R. Valentien
11480 N. Torrey Pines Road, La Jolla, 858-453-4220;
www. lodgeattorreypines.com
La Jolla's Lodge at Torrey Pines may be best known for its golf, but its much-lauded restaurant, A.R. Valentien, is a show-stopper. Named after an impressionist California artist, the dining room is a showcase of stained glass lighting and Mission-style furnishings with large windows overlooking the 18th hole. Chef Jeff Jackson delivers stand-out traditional American cooking focusing on the quality of ingredients. Settle in and sample dishes like local swordfish with toasted orzo, clams, roasted peppers and tapenade crostini. The outstanding creations of West Coast producers dot the superlative cheese list, so be sure to save room for a taste.
American menu. Dinner. Reservations recommended. $$$

JACK'S LA JOLLA DINING ROOM

★★★★Jack's La Jolla Dining Room

7863 Girard Ave., La Jolla, 858-465-8111; www.jackslajolla.com

Part of a cluster of restaurants and lounges all under one roof in downtown
La Jolla (Jack's Grille and Jack's Ocean Room are the other two dining
outlets and there are multiple lounges), the Dining Room is undoubtedly the
star of the group. Chef Tony DiSalvo gives San Diegoans some of the best
food in the area. The menu looks traditional at first, but look again—dishes
include lobster with Kaffir lime juice and sticks of Fuji apple, or spice-crusted
black sea bass with Japanese eggplant. The room is crisp and elegant,
with tall banquettes to snuggle up in as well as white linen-topped tables
for lingering over decadent desserts like chocolate caramel custard.
Seafood menu. Dinner. Reservations recommended. $$$

★★★★Laurel

505 Laurel St., San Diego, 619-239-2222; www.laurelrestaurant.com

Make a grand entrance down a sweeping, wrought-iron staircase into
this sleek and sexy 3,200-square-foot dining room. The décor, a glam-
orous update of traditional colonial that pairs houndstooth chairs with
deconstructed crystal chandeliers and acid-green tufted banquettes, is
as eye-catching as the stylish crowd that gathers around the bar each
evening to sip cocktails such as sparkling cosmopolitans (which are spiked
with champagne). The food is rustic, contemporary and French; signature
dishes include salmon with white asparagus and paella loaded with local
seafood such as rock shrimp and mussels. The restaurant's stellar wine list
features selections from across the globe. Laurel also hosts some of the
best live jazz musicians in town, making the bar a lively spot to unwind and
make new friends.
French, Mediterranean menu. Dinner. Bar. Casual attire. Valet parking. $$$

Extraordinary Desserts

*2929 Fifth Ave., San Diego, 619-294-2123; 1430 Union St., San Diego,
619-294-7001; www.extraordinarydesserts.com*

You can't leave San Diego without trying one of the best dessert places in
town. It will be a sweet sendoff from a trip downtown and is an ideal after-
dinner locale. Paris-trained pastry chef Karen Krasne returned to her native

San Diego to craft elegant desserts at two locations near downtown including her best-selling Gianduia (dark chocolate cake layers dressed up with hazelnut buttercream and boysenberry preserve). Try the lemon praline if you want something light and bright. Krasne also offers house-made ice cream and sorbets, with flavors updated daily. Make it a whole meal with the daily selection of paninis and salads.

Dessert menu. Breakfast, lunch, dinner, late-night. Casual attire. $

Gelateria Frizzante

1025 Prospect St., La Jolla, 858-454-5798
After a day in the sun, you simply must stop by this popular gelato parlor located just steps away from La Jolla Cove. Cool down with a cantaloupe gelato or a black-and-white stracciatella (chocolate chips in vanilla gelato).

Gelato menu. Lunch, dinner. $

The Living Room

1010 Prospect St., La Jolla, 858-459-1187;
www.livingroomcafe.com/lajolla.html
This popular coffeehouse is a convenient haven for college students and locals who enjoy its style, ambience and oversized, dark wood tables—not to mention the coffee drinks, pastries and sandwiches of La Jolla's signature quality.

Coffee menu. Breakfast, lunch, dinner, late-night. Casual attire. $

see

La Jolla Shores

8200 Camino del Oro, La Jolla;
www.sandiego.gov/lifeguards/beaches/shores.shtml
This beach is a favorite among locals for its tame shore. Parents need not worry, for La Jolla Shores is known for mild waves and is ideal for children who can swim in shallow waters. The beach also has several barbeque pits for evening bonfires. The sand is silky with glints of false gold and is distinctly darker than the sands of beaches farther north in Orange County and Los Angeles.

La Jolla Cove

1100 Coast Blvd., La Jolla, 619-221-8901;
www.sandiego.gov/lifeguards/beaches/cove.shtml
An ideal place for picnicking, the La Jolla Cove provides a marvelous backdrop of the Pacific Ocean and sandy cliffs, and is an ideal place to see the water crash against the craggy rocks at the cove's

LA JOLLA COVE

GASLAMP QUARTER

point. The churning sea perfumes the air with the scent of seaweed. After taking a walk along the sidewalk, relax on the lawn and drink in the sun. Located at the southern edge of the San Diego-La Jolla Underwater Park, the cove is an ecologically protected area. The tiny beach is a great place to sunbathe, snorkel or scuba dive and check out the seals, which are often seen sunbathing on the Cove's rocky edge. Divers can enjoy visibility of more than 30 feet and the waters are ideal for photography. Daily.

see in san deigo

Aerospace Museum and Hall of Fame
2001 Pan American Plaza, San Diego, 619-234-8291;
www.aerospacemuseum.org
Learn about the extraordinary accomplishments of the world's leading aviation pioneers, including the Wright Brothers, Amelia Earhart, Neil Armstrong and others. Admission is $15 for adults and $6 for kids under 12. Memorial Day-Labor Day 10 a.m.-5:30 p.m., rest of the year 10 a.m.-4:30 p.m.

Balboa Park
1549 El Prado, San Diego, 619-239-0512; www.balboapark.org
Located in the heart of the city, this 1,200-acre park includes galleries, museums, theaters, restaurants, recreational facilities and miles of garden walks. Daily.

Cabrillo National Monument
1800 Cabrillo Memorial Drive, San Diego, 619-557-5450; www.nps.gov/cabr
In late autumn of 1542, explorer Juan Rodriguez Cabrillo and his crew arrived at what he called a very good enclosed port, the San Diego Harbor. Today, his statue looks out over one of the most beautiful views in all of San Diego. The grounds of this national park include a historic lighthouse. From late December through mid-March, natives come to this site to watch the annual migration of Pacific gray whales. Don't miss the coastal tide pools, particularly exciting during winter's low tides, when the sea pushes back to reveal a unique world of marine plants and animals in little pockets of the earth. Daily.

Coronado Island

1100 Orange Ave., Coronado, 619-437-8788; www.coronadovisitorcenter.com
Coronado is a place to leave the car behind. Once across the bridge, park and walk past homes with gardens of flowers native only to this part of the country, and through the quaint stores of Orange Avenue. Hop the ferry to Ferry Landing Marketplace, a center of fine dining, specialty shops, art galleries and bike rentals. There's also a waterfront park, beach, family amusement center and Farmers' Market every Tuesday from 2:30-6 p.m.

Gaslamp Quarter

Downtown, 619-233-5227; www.gaslamp.org
Once the city's business center at the turn of the century, today many Victorian buildings in this nearly 17-block historic district are under restoration. The area is packed with bars and restaurants.

Horton Plaza

324 Horton Plaza, San Diego, 619-239-8180; www.westfield.com/hortonplaza
Sixteen years of research went into the design of this whimsical, multilevel shopping mall with more than 140 specialty shops, department stores and restaurants. The black concrete and narrow walkways were patterned after those found in European marketplaces, and many merchants display their goods on carts. Monday-Friday 10 a.m.-9 p.m., Saturday 10 a.m.-8 p.m., Sunday 11 a.m.-7 p.m.

Pacific Beach bike trail ▪ Del Mar Beach ▪ San Diego's Ocean Beach ▪ Dining alfresco in San Diego

drive

Eventually, as Sunday afternoon begins to wane, it's time to head back. You can re-live the drive to San Diego by heading back to L.A. via the same route, or you can take new ones you didn't have time for on the way down (see chapter 7). Either way, you'll want to be sure to take the Highway 1 detour from Orange County to the outskirts of L.A., as there's no better scenic route than the famous Pacific Coast Highway.

CHAPTER 4
LOS ANGELES TO SANTA BARBARA

Santa Barbara is only two hours from Los Angeles, but it might as well be a world away. Often called the "American Riviera," the historic city, an old Spanish mission town, is sandwiched between the Pacific Coast and the mountains of the Santa Ynez Valley. The luxurious town and its surrounding areas (where lavish estates have been snapped up by Brad Pitt, Oprah Winfrey and Ellen DeGeneres), are not only stunning, there are activities available for every kind of traveler. Adventure junkies can take advantage of beach and mountain sports like surfing, horseback riding and fishing. Foodies have their pick of the finest restaurants, authentic Mexican taquerias and fresh fish and farmer's markets. And intellectual folk can shop for arts and antiques and go wine tasting in the valley. The weather is also spectacular, with temperatures during the day averaging between 65 and 80 degrees, making it the perfect getaway anytime of year.

HOTEL BEL-AIR

starting out

Make like a movie star and start your weekend with a restful night's sleep at the classic **Hotel Bel-Air** (*701 Stone Canyon Road, Los Angeles, 310-472-1211, 888-897-2804; www.hotelbelair.com*) or at the deliciously pink **Beverly Hills Hotel** (*9641 Sunset Blvd., Beverly Hills, 310-276-2251, 888-897-2804; www.beverlyhillshotel.com*).

drive

There are two ways to get to Santa Barbara from the city of angels. There is the "fast way" up Highway 101 (which can quickly turn into a churn with traffic coming out of the city) or there is the scenic route up the Pacific Coast Highway (CA-1). With a full weekend ahead of you, why not do both? Try taking the 101 to Santa Barbara, then take PCH on the way back to prolong your weekend getaway. The 101 just outside of Los Angeles isn't very exciting until you get to Oxnard, which is about an hour from L.A. Even though the drive to Santa Barbara is relatively short, there are a couple of fun stops along the way.

see

Ronald Reagan Presidential Library

40 Presidential Drive, Simi Valley, 800-410-8354; www.reaganfoundation.org
Ronald Reagan owned a ranch high in the Santa Barbara Mountains. Stop by his comprehensive library, located just eight miles off the 101 (take CA-23 North toward Fillmore and follow signs). Perched on a mountaintop with views of the mountains, valleys and Pacific Ocean, this 100-acre site has exhibits that follow Reagan from childhood to the glamorous world of Hollywood stardom, to his inauguration as the 40th President of the United States. Key events of his two terms are revealed through documents, photographs and artifacts. This is a must-see for any history buff or future presidential hopeful—donkey, elephant or otherwise. Daily 10 a.m.-5 p.m.

Camarillo Premium Outlets

740 E. Ventura Blvd., Camarillo,805-445-8520; www.premiumoutlets.com
It may not be Rodeo Drive, but you can't beat the price tags. Just a mile from exit 55 on the 101, the Camarillo outlets offer 120 factory outlet stores,

including Barney's, Saks Fifth Avenue, Theory and Michael Kors. Open Monday-Saturday 10 a.m.-9 p.m., Sunday 10 a.m.-8 p.m.

drive

After power shopping and boning up on your American history, it's time for a little r&r. Continue cruising north on the 101 until you hit the coastal city of Ventura. Here, you'll follow signs for the scenic Highway 33 north toward Ojai.

stop

Located 15 miles inland from the Pacific Coast, Ojai is a small, tranquil community surrounded by 500,000 acres of picturesque mountains, green valleys and streams, and has reportedly been the backdrop for Hollywood productions from the *Bionic Woman* to videos by the band Green Day. It's also known for its adorable downtown, which has world-class art galleries, boutiques, cafés, restaurants, bookstores, a small park and a movie theater, and a handful of luxury spas. It's the perfect place to stop for a meal, or for an overnight stay at the **Ojai Valley Inn & Spa** (*905 Country Club Road, Ojai, 805-646-1111; www. ojairesort.com*), which looks just like the kind of California ranch at which presidents are always photographed riding their horses. In June, the area hosts the Ojai Music Festival, showcasing classical artists, and the Ojai Wine Festival, showcasing the area's local vineyards.

eat

★★★L'Auberge

314 El Paseo Road, Ojai, 805-646-2288

Nestled among oak trees and situated in a rustic cabin built in 1905, chef Christian Shaffer serves up fresh French/American country cuisine while you watch incredible sunsets over the Topa Topa Mountains. The monthly changing menu includes entrées such as oysters, clams, lamb, oxtail and venison. Continental, French menu. Dinner, Sunday brunch. Closed Monday-Tuesday. Casual attire. Reservations recommended. Outdoor seating. $$

★★★The Ranch House

S. Lomita Ave., Ojai, 805-646-2360; www.theranchhouse.com

One of the forerunners of California cuisine, The Ranch House made a name for itself many decades ago by offering simple, made-from-scratch dishes—many of them vegetarian—that burst with fresh flavors. The years have seen some changes, but many things remain the same here. Fresh herbs from the garden are still used in all the recipes, and the loaves of bread that are served to patrons (and sold to locals) are still made fresh daily. Dishes like wild mushroom strudel and grilled diver scallops with sweet corn sauce have been keeping guests coming back, and its garden setting with quiet streams and lush foliage make it a perfect spot for a relaxing lunch.

American menu. Dinner, Sunday brunch. Closed Monday. Children's menu. Outdoor seating. $$$

Suzanne's Cuisine

502 W. Ojai Ave., Ojai, 805-640-1961; www.suzannescuisine.com

This cozy restaurant, run by a mother/daughter duo, serves comfort food infused with Asian, Indian, French and Mexican spices. For lunch, there is a large selection of fresh salads and sandwiches (the juicy chicken sandwich tasted like it had just come off the grill), while dinner focuses on pasta and seafood

FOUR SEASONS RESORT
THE BILTMORE

dishes. Seating is available on a flower-laden patio. Continental menu. Lunch, dinner. Closed Tuesday. Bar. Casual attire. Reservations recommended. Outdoor seating. $$

drive

After leaving Ojai and getting back on the 101 in Ventura, the only places to stop are a few quaint towns lurking on the outskirts of Santa Barbara, like Summerland and Carpinteria, which is known for its orchid hothouses and avocado-laden hills, but also offers kayak and surfboard rentals right off a convenient exit named Santa Claus Lane. But with the deep blue Pacific Ocean on your left and stunning mountain vistas on your right, there's nothing to complain about. Suddenly, a few miles from the final destination, you'll come over a vista and see the valley of Santa Barbara in the distance—and it's obvious why it's called "The American Riviera."

The sky is so blue it's almost purple. The beach is lined with palm trees, and the lush, green foothills are dotted with beautiful, Spanish-style homes. In fact, just before you arrive at the Santa Barbara exits, you'll pass the ritzy enclave of Montecito, perhaps best known for being the summer vacation town of Oprah Winfrey, whose massive estate is located here.

After getting off at the Garden Street exit, a quick left brings you down to Santa Barbara's waterfront district. After taking a right on West Cabrillo Boulevard, which is lined with charming hotels, seafood restaurants and historic Stearns Wharf, take another right onto State Street, which will bring you into the center of town, essentially an impeccably clean outdoor mall with high-end shops, world-renowned art galleries and open-air restaurants, cafes and bars. The city's historic buildings and Mission District are also located nearby.

stop

Tourists have flocked to Santa Barbara for it's beautiful Mediterranean weather, downtown beaches and Spanish-influenced architecture. Nicknamed the "South Coast" due to its south-facing coastline, Santa Barbara boasts views from sunrise to sunset and is home to countless celebrity estates and palatial properties. With a Mission revival style of architecture adopted throughout the city, there is a distinct aura in Santa Barbara. The ordinances passed against billboards and outdoor advertising

BACARA SPA AND POOL

BACARA RESORT FITNESS TRAIL

add to its unique clutter-free atmosphere. Explore the famed Santa Barbara mission and other national historic landmarks, or plan your trip for late June and attend the Summer Solstice Parade, drawing more than 100,000 for the city's most festive event.

stay

★★★★Bacara Resort & Spa

8301 Hollister Ave., Santa Barbara, 805-968-0100, 877-422-4245; www.bacararesort.com

With its spectacular setting overlooking the Pacific and dash of old-time Hollywood glamour, this resort is a jetsetter's fantasy. The luxurious rooms include Frette linens and private balconies, and service is attentive enough to make anyone feel like a celebrity. There are three infinity-edge pools on the grounds surrounded by 26 private cabanas. And the spa has everything to help guests relax and feel pampered, from citrus-avocado body polishes to the Bacara Body Melt using ylang ylang and eucalyplus oils. You'll also find golf, tennis, yoga, meditation and delicious California cuisine in the restaurant.

360 rooms. Restaurant, bar. Children's activity center. Pool. Golf. Tennis. Business center. Pets accepted. $$$$

★★★★Four Seasons Resort The Biltmore Santa Barbara

1260 Channel Drive, Santa Barbara, 805-969-2261; www.fourseasons.com

Situated on 20 lush acres on the Pacific Ocean, the resort pays tribute to the region's Spanish colonial history with its red-tiled roof, arches and hacienda-style main building. The guest rooms, located both in the main building and in separate cottages, feature a relaxed Spanish-colonial décor and include down pillows and luxe bathrobes. Crisp white cabanas line the sparkling pool. Besides offering a full menu of massages, facials and body wraps, the world-class spa incorporates botanicals from the gardens into its treatments. Dinner at the oceanfront Bella Vista restaurant is a special treat, particularly if you get a table close to one of the outdoor firepits.

207 rooms. High-speed Internet access. Two restaurants, bar. Spa. Tennis. Business center. Pets accepted. $$$$

SAN YSIDRO RANCH

★★★★San Ysidro Ranch, a Rosewood Resort

900 San Ysidro Lane, Montecito, 805-969-5046, 800-368-6788; www.sanysidroranch.com

Settle in at this 550-acre resort and you'll see why John and Jackie Kennedy spent part of their honeymoon here, tucked away in the foothills of Montecito. Lushly planted acres are filled with fragrant flowers and plants, and stunning vistas of the Pacific Ocean and the Channel Islands can be seen in the distance. The bungalows, with their cozy blend of overstuffed chintz armchairs, oriental rugs and vaulted, wood-clad ceilings, provide luxuries like wood-burning fireplaces and Frette linens. Exceptional cuisine is a hallmark of this resort, and the two restaurants here provide charming settings for the imaginative food.

41 rooms. High-speed Internet access. Restaurant, bar. Pool. Tennis. Pets accepted. $$$$

eat

★★★Bouchon

9 W. Victoria St., Santa Barbara, 805-730-1160; www.bouchonsantabarbara.com

This critically acclaimed French restaurant prides itself on using the freshest local ingredients available including fish from the Santa Barbara Channel, produce from the surrounding countryside, meats and poultry from local micro-ranches and wine from the Santa Ynez Valley. Order the pan-seared scallops with herb risotto, or try bourbon and maple-glazed duck. The molten "lava" chocolate cake is a sweet ending to any meal. French menu. Dinner. Reservations recommended. $$$

★★★Downey's

1305 State St., Santa Barbara, 805-966-5006; www.downeyssb.com

The menu at Downey's, which changes constantly, offers appetizers such as the Santa Barbara mussels with sweet corn and a chili vinaigrette or

homemade duck sausage with lentils. Signature entrées include grilled lamb loin or local sea bass with a ragout of prawns and spring vegetables. The relaxed setting combines to make it a local favorite.
Continental menu. Dinner. Closed Monday. Reservations recommended. $$$

★★★★Miró at Bacara Resort
8301 Hollister Ave., Santa Barbara, 805-571-4204, 877-422-4245;
www.bacararesort.com
Santa Barbara's luxurious Bacara Resort is home to the delightful Miró Restaurant. Joan Miró-style artwork, deep red dining chairs, a contemporary carpet and fantastic views of the Pacific Ocean set the scene, while the chef creates masterful renditions of traditional Spanish cooking such as oak-grilled lamb chops with aged Sherry and pan-roasted lobster with oven-roasted tomatoes. The 12,000-bottle wine cellar has something to match each meal. For a more casual alternative, the Miró Bar and Lounge features homemade sangria and tapas
Basque Catalonian menu. Dinner. Closed Sunday-Monday. Bar. Business casual attire. Reservations recommended. Valet parking. Outdoor seating. $$$$

Restaurant at San Ysidro Ranch • Soaking tubs at San Ysidro Ranch • Guest room • Appetizer from Elements •

Elements
129 E. Anapamu St., Santa Barbara, 805-884-9218;
www.elementsrestaurantandbar.com
The inventive cuisine at Elements is best enjoyed in the fresh air; you can have lunch, brunch and dinner on the patio here while viewing a national landmark, the Santa Barbara Courthouse and Sunken Gardens. Specialties include the grilled Ahi tuna wrap with wasabi mayo and cinnamon spiced duck confit risotto.
Pacific menu. Lunch, dinner, Sunday brunch. Reservations recommended. Outdoor seating. $$

La Super-Rica Taqueria
622 N. Milpas St., Santa Barbara, 805-963-4940
Don't let the funky, rundown shack-like exterior deter you from sampling Santa Barbara's most famous authentic Mexican food, a favorite of gourmand Julia Child. The lines are endless but the fresh tamales and cheap

FOUR SEASONS RESORT
THE BILTMORE

OLIO E LIMONE
WALNUT SALAD

tacos—handmade corn tortillas filled with carne asada, marinated pork, chicken, occasionally Dover sole and more—are beyond delicious and well worth the wait.

Mexican menu. Lunch, dinner. Closed Wenesday. Casual attrire. Cash only. $

Olio e Limone

11 West Victoria St., Santa Barbara,
805-899-2699; www.olioelimone.com

Another favorite of once-local Julia Child, this upscale yet low-key restaurant is the place where locals and out of towners go for the best Italian in the area. Signature dishes include the spaghetti alla bottarga, duck breast, panna cotta and pear carpaccio.

Italian menu. Lunch, dinner. Reservations recommended. $$

Sambo's

216 W. Cabrillo Blvd., Santa Barbara,
805-965-3269; www.sambosrestaurant.com

For the best breakfast on the beach, sit on the outdoor patio at Sambo's and order up a plate of fluffy pancakes, a delicious omelet or a breakfast burrito, made with fresh local avocado.

Breakfast menu. Breakfast, lunch. Outdoor seating. $

Santa Barbara Shellfish Company

230 Stearns Wharf, Santa Barbara, 805-966-6676;
www.sbfishhouse.com

If you head to historic Stearns Wharf, be sure to walk all the way to the very end of the pier or you'll miss this great fish shack. Grab a stool at the small bar inside and order up the best of Santa Barbara clam chowder, fresh oysters and mussels, or the whole shebang in the Cioppino: mussels, clams, shrimp, crab and scallops all steaming in a giant bread bowl.

Seafood menu. Lunch, dinner. Outdoor seating. $

Tupelo Junction Cafe

1218 State St., Santa Barbara, 805-899-3100;
www.tupelojunction.com

For a hearty, homestyle breakfast, try the southern-style-meets eclectic home cooking at Tupelo Junction. Don't-miss menu items include the cinnamon apple beignets, old-fashioned buttermilk biscuits slathered in gravy, and poached eggs on crispy crab cakes with fresh avocado.

American menu. Breakfast, lunch, dinner. Reservations recommended. $

BACARA SPA

spa

★★★★Bacara Spa

8301 Hollister Ave., Santa Barbara, 805-968-0100, 877-422-4245;
www.bacararesort.com

With the Pacific Ocean on one side and the Santa Ynez Mountains on the other, Bacara is all about location. A fitness center, a saline-filled pool and secluded nooks for sunbathing flank more than 30 treatment rooms and indoor and outdoor massage stations. The spa offers an intriguing selection of global healing regimens, and an Eastern Origin menu, which features options such as reiki and shiatsu massages. The rugged terrain of the Santa Ynez Mountains is the perfect place for a rigorous walk, run or hike. Clay tennis courts, pools almost too pretty to swim in and yoga on the beach are just a few of the other fitness options.

★★★★Spa at Four Seasons Resort The Biltmore Santa Barbara

1260 Channel Drive, Santa Barbara, 805-969-2261, 800-819-5053;
www.fourseasons.com

Pure luxury sums up the look and feel of this oceanfront spa, whose design echoes the Spanish colonial style of the Four Seasons Resort in which it's located. Treatments rooms are more residential than spa-like, with kiva fireplaces, plush treatment tables and mission-style furniture. The signature avocado citrus wrap combines fruit extracts with sea salts and clay to hydrate and heal. The oxy-mist is another signature treatment, and the stone therapy uses both hot and cold stones to target the nervous system. Hair and styling services, manicures, pedicures and makeup are also available.

see

Santa Barbara Botanic Garden

1212 Mission Canyon Road, Santa Barbara, 805-682-4726; www.sbbg.org

Set on 40 acres in Santa Barbara, this decades-old botanic garden allows visitors to traverse its 5.5 miles of walking paths through its 1,000-plus plant types as well as its vast herbarium including roughly 143,000 preserved species. While the botanic garden is best visited in warmer months, it is open year round and demonstrates the variety of plant life in southern California during all months. Open March-October 9 a.m.-6 p.m., November-February 9 a.m.-5 p.m.

El Paseo de Santa Barbara

900 State St.
Pick up a few stylin' souvenirs while you're away. Built between 1921 and 1924, this block of galleries, restaurants, and clothing and gift shops is considered the oldest shopping center in California, and a Santa Barbara landmark.

East Beach

Sun worshippers will love this picturesque stretch of sand located on East Cabrillo Boulevard. Amenities include a full beach house, snack bar, volleyball courts, play area for children and bike/rollerblading paths. It also hosts the Santa Barbara Art Show on Sundays.

Santa Barbara Botanic Garden ▪ Farmers Market ▪ Mission Santa Barbara ▪ Lake Cachuma

Market Forays with Laurence Hauben

805-259-7229; www.marketforays.com
For a foodie exploration of Santa Barbara, take an all-day cooking class with Laurence Hauber, the leader of Santa Barbara's Slow Food movement and an editor at *Food & Home* magazine. Start off the day at the local farmers' market picking fresh seafood right off the boat; select the freshest and most fragrant fruits and vegetables from neighboring farms (sometimes right off the tree or vine); and then head to an artisanal cheese store before settling into a lovely kitchen to prepare dinner. Finish the day by enjoying your five-course meal, while learning all about the local wine parings that match. Fees vary.

Mission Santa Barbara

2201 Laguna St., Santa Barbara, 805-682-4149; www.sbmission.org
This unofficial city landmark was built in 1786 as the tenth of the California missions to be founded by the Spanish Franciscans. A climb to the top of the mission's two towers provides a breathtaking view of Santa Barbara. Secular and non-secular activities take place in the mission daily. Self-guided tours operate from 9 a.m. to 5 p.m.

Museum of Art

1130 State St., Santa Barbara, 805-963-4364; www.sbma.net
The Santa Barbara Museum of Art is a privately funded, not-for-profit institution. Here you'll find cultural and educational activities as well as internationally recognized collections and exhibitions ranging from antiqui-

STERNS WHARF

ties to contemporary art and spanning the globe. Don't miss the works on paper collection, the largest collection within the museum. Tuesday-Sunday 11 a.m.-5 p.m. Closed Monday. Admission is free on Sunday.

Santa Barbara Certified Farmers Market

805-962-5354; www.sbfarmersmarket.org
Each Saturday, local farmers head to the main marketplace in Santa Barbara's downtown to display a colorful bounty of agricultural products grown right in the city's backyard. (The market moves to different locations in the area during the week.) You'll find seasonal diversity year-round, rain or shine. Music and entertainment enliven the markets and enriches the ambiance. Closed Monday. Check the Web site for daily locations.

Santa Barbara Royal Presidio

123 E. Canon Perdido St., Santa Barbara, 805-965-0093;
www.sbthp.org/presidio.htm
A former military headquarters and government center, this fortress was founded on April 21, 1782. It was the Spanish's center for defense against Native American inhabitants of the area, and two corners of the Presidio's main quadrangle remain. Today they stand as part of a state park and visitors can see what the living structures for soldiers based here were like. The location was carefully chosen as a place of outlook and defense. Open 10:30 a.m. to 4:30 p.m. daily.

Stearns Wharf and Ty Warner Sea Center

State Street and the Pacific Ocean, 805-962-2526; www.sbnature.org
Once a major shipping hub for all of southern California, this pier, built in 1872, has dramatic views of Santa Barbara, and is now home to several fresh seafood restaurants, including the delicious Santa Barbara Shellfish Company and gift shops. The Ty Warner Sea Center, part of the Santa Barbara Museum of Natural History, is an interactive marine education facility where visitors have the opportunity to work like scientists, sample and test

ocean water, study animal behavior and examine microscopic marine life. Daily 10 a.m. -5 p.m.

drive

After a day of sampling vintage grapes (make sure you have a designated driver), you can coast back to Santa Barbara on the beautiful backcountry Highway 154 (The San Marcos Pass), which winds down through the valley. Along the way, you'll pass the 3,250-acre **Cachuma Lake Recreational Area,** the perfect place to stop and take pictures of the crystal blue waters and mountains, or simply stretch your legs. Campsites, rental boats and fishing equipment and licenses are also available. Down the road a few miles, if you're still hungry or just want to listen to great live music, don't miss the historic **Cold Spring Tavern** *(5995 Stagecoach Main, Santa Barbara, 805-967-0066; www.coldspringtavern.com)*, a stage coach stop built in The San Marcos Pass in 1865 that's still lit by kerosene lamps. It's a favorite haunt of local bikers and celebrities—but it's also not marked well, so keep your eyes peeled for the turnoff at Stagecoach Road. Fifteen miles further down Highway 154 and you'll be back in Santa Barbara.

After spending a luxe weekend in gorgeous Santa Barbara, it's hard to imagine heading back to the hustle and bustle of L.A. So take your time. On the way out of SB on the 101, stop at **Rincon Point**, a public beach and park that is widely considered the best surfing spot in California. There, you can eat whatever snacks you have left and watch the surfers ride the waves. Rincon Point is not well marked, so keep a look out for the Bates Road exit, which will lead you straight to the ocean.

Head south afterward but instead of taking the 101 all the way back to L.A., consider taking the scenic route along the Pacific Coast Highway (CA-1), which you can pick up in Oxnard. As you approach Oxnard on the 101, look for the Pacific Coast Highway exit sign. Unfortunately, upon exiting you'll drive through about 10 miles of strip malls in Oxnard, but when you finally hit the famous stretch of highway, you'll realize it was worth it. PCH is an incredible drive along the Pacific Ocean that takes you through the 27-mile-long city of Malibu. Along the way, you'll see gigantic, oceanfront homes (many of which are owned by A-list stars). You can also stop at several public beaches along the way, where you'll spot surfers, kite boarders and windsurfers. And if you're still hungry or thirsty, there are several excellent seaside shanty restaurants along the way, including **Moonshadows** (*20356 Pacific Coast Highway, Malibu, 310-456-3010; www. moonshadowsmalibu.com;* where Mel Gibson reportedly partied before his fateful DUI arrest) and **Gladstone's** (*17300 Pacific Coast Highway, Malibu, 310-454-3474; www.gladstones.com)* for fresh seafood or a delicious breakfast. The Pacific Coast Highway comes to an end in Santa Monica—and when you hit that inevitable awful traffic on the 101, your road rage may rear its ugly head. Luckily, you've got that case of Santa Barbara vino to keep the memories fresh.

WINE TASTING

Day trip: Solvang and the Santa Barbara Wine Country

While Santa Barbara offers plenty to do, a half-day or all-day road trip to the village of Solvang—the Danish Capital of America—and the Santa Ynez Valley's thousands of acres of award-winning vineyards (which were highlighted in the Oscar-nominated movie *Sideways*) is a must.

Hop in the car and drive northwest on the 101 for about 32 miles until you reach Highway 246, which will bring you east to Solvang. This authentic Danish community offers quaint inns, Scandinavian restaurants that serve delicacies like aebleskiver and smorgaasbord, The Hans Christian Andersen museum and dozens of shops that sell everything from Old World antiques to homemade candy.

After you've had your fill of Danish delicacies, take Highway 246 to Alamo-Pintado Road, which will lead you north to Los Olivos and the Santa Ynez Wine Loop. This three-mile triangle features about 10 vineyards, including the charming Buttonwood Farm and Blackjack Ranch. In between tastings, you'll pass roadside stands selling apples, avocados, peaches, flowers, lavender—even whole pigs. Midway through the Wine Loop, you'll pass through the delightful town of Los Olivos, where you can stop for a bite to eat at a outdoor bistro, like the Los Olivos Café, Panino or Patrick's Side Street Café, peruse the local art galleries or visit more tasting rooms. And be sure to check out Jedlicka's Saddlery (*2883 Grand Avenue, Los Olivos, 805-688-2626; www.jedlicka. com)*, an authentic Western store that has catered to ranchers and trail riders—reportedly including President Reagan—for more than 70 years.

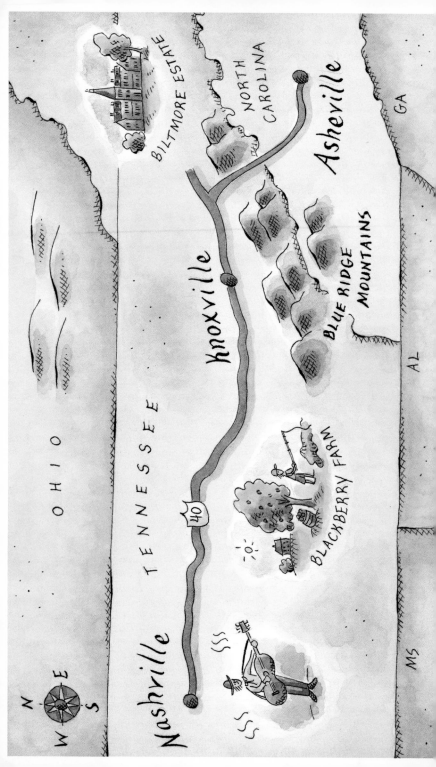

CHAPTER 5
NASHVILLE TO ASHEVILLE

Luxury travel might not be the first thing that comes to mind when you think Tennessee, but this upscale road trip from the sizzling state capital to neighboring North Carolina is guaranteed to change your mind. You'll find all the pampering, haute cuisine and luxury accommodations of the coasts, but with the added bonus of a little Southern charm and gentility. Though spring and fall are the preferred times to travel, the lack of snow in the region makes this a viable winter getaway as well. Start in Nashville and head east to Walland, home of Blackberry Farm (just southeast of Knoxville). After a night in one of the most luxurious country inns in the nation, make your way across the state line to Asheville, North Carolina and to the largest estate in the United States: The famed Biltmore Estate.

starting out

Start your weekend with an evening at the Mobil Five-Star **Hermitage Hotel** (*231 Sixth Ave. N., Nashville, 615-244-3121, 888-888-9414; www.the-hermitagehotel.com*). Opened in 1910 and renovated in 2003, this glorious downtown hotel offers white-glove service, spacious guest rooms with elegant traditional furnishings and fine dining at the Capitol Grille, one of Nashville's most popular restaurants.

drive

The three-and-a-half hour drive from Nashville to Walland is simple, as it's a straight shot on Interstate 40 to Knoxville, which gets you 90 percent of the way there. Traffic on I-40 (a four-lane expressway) can be heavy during rush hour, but once you're outside the Nashville city limits, the landscape flattens and becomes beautifully rural and expansive. While many roadside rest stops present the typical burger and fries options of any major highway, golf enthusiasts may want to pull off at exit 320. Here, you'll find the town of **Crossville**, known by locals as the golf capital of Tennessee—and with good reason. More than a dozen courses (including several championship courses) amounting to a whopping 200-plus holes adorn the town's famed Cumberland Plateau.

Suite at the Hermitage Hotel • Capitol Grille • Lobby at the Hermitage Hotel • Nashville Music Hall of Fame

With your clubs securely tucked in the trunk, continue east on I-40 to Knoxville, a town of about 180,000 and the former capital of Tennessee. Follow signs for Highway 129 (you will be about 25 minutes from Walland), and take it south toward Marysville. As you pass the Knoxville airport, stay in the left lanes when the highway splits and keep your eyes peeled for Highway 321 toward Townsend. Take Highway 321 out of Maryville and continue for nine miles until you see the Foothills Parkway entrance sign, where you will hang a right onto West Millers Cover Road and follow signs for Blackberry Farm.

stop

Perched in the northwestern foothills of the Great Smoky Mountains and boasting a population just over 3,700 residents, Walland exemplifies the tranquil beauty of the southeast. Hiking trails, rippling creeks and verdant valleys abound and by nightfall, a symphony of natural sounds is all you can hear from your heavenly accomodations.

NASHVILLE RIVER

stay

★ ★ ★ ★ Blackberry Farm

1471 W. Millers Cove Road, Walland, 800-648-4252; www.blackberryfarm.com
From the moment you pass through the front gates where you'll trade
your vehicle for a golf cart to use for the remainder of the weekend, to
the time you leave this splendid resort, you'll be transported to a world
of unassuming extravagance. Nestled at the foot of the Great Smoky
Mountains, Blackberry Farm is the perfect blend of luxury accommodations
and rural seclusion. From the picturesque and beautifully landscaped
grounds and idyllic farmhouse setting to the impeccable service and
amenities, Blackberry Farm provides the backdrop for a relaxing
experience. There are a variety of unique accommodations, most of which
are housed in small luxurious cottages throughout the forested grounds,
complete with wood burning fireplaces and stocked pantries. Breakfast
and lunch are served daily in the main house dining room and dinner is
served in the new food and wine venue, The Barn. Since the room rate is
inclusive of all your meals, you will want to make sure you don't miss a
bite, as the food here is world-class. Spend a lazy afternoon on the dock
overlooking the pond or reading a book in a hammock as the sound of the
rushing creek goes by. Or explore one of six trails on the 4,200-acre estate.
Not to worry if you grow tired; that's where the golf carts come in handy.
44 rooms. Children over 10 years only. Restaurant. Fitness center. Pool.
Tennis. Airport transportation available. $$$

eat

Blackberry Farm

1471 W. Millers Cove Road, Walland, 800-648-4252; www.blackberryfarm.com
Designed in the same country-meets-luxury style that Blackberry Farm
exhibits in its rooms, its two restaurants allow guests to sample regionally-
inspired dishes on a nightly basis. Executive chef John Fleer's "Foothills
Cuisine" uses the freshest ingredients from Blackberry Farm's onsite
heirloom garden and its own house-made cheese, eggs and honey. Diners

choose from three menus: A chef's tasting menu, an à la carte menu or a garden tasting menu, with additional attention to calorie-counting guests. Each day, lunch is served as a picnic for you to take along as you explore the estate. Or, if you're checking out, staff will package your lunch to take with you. On Sundays, a continental breakfast is whisked up to your room; brunch is also served at 10 a.m.

American menu. Breakfast, lunch, dinner. Casual attire. $$$

spa

Farmhouse Spa

1471 W. Millers Cove Road, Walland, 800-648-4252;
www.blackberryfarm.com
Located within a historic farmhouse on the grounds, the Farmhouse Aveda concept spa provides a mini oasis within the farm itself. Here you'll find everything from massage treatments to manicures to rejuvenating facials, but the place is small (part of the overall charm), so book before you arrive if possible. Depending on where your room is located, you can walk to the spa, but after your treatments (and you're feeling like Jell-O), staff will offer you a ride back to the main house.

see

Cooking School and Epicurean Events

The Foothill Cuisine at Blackberry Farm promises to satisfy your inner foodie, and you can learn some of the house secrets at one of Blackberry Farm's 20 yearly cooking school and wine events. Contact the hotel directly to inquire about specific programs and events, as space is limited. Such notable chefs as Grant Achatz, Thomas Keller and Bradley Ogden have made or will

make appearances at the culinary counter. Maple Cottage; times and dates vary.

Horseback riding

The best way to explore the grounds of Blackberry Farm and the Great Smoky Mountains is on horseback. Two-hour, half-day, full-day trail rides and clinics are available along with private rides, which can be reserved in advance. Daily, 9 a.m. and 2 p.m.

Fly-fishing

Blackberry Farm offers a variety of fishing locations as well as fly-fishing equipment and instruction on property grounds and in the neighboring Great Smoky Mountains. Don't worry if you forgot your lucky rod. Orvis-endorsed guides will provide everything you'll need for a successful outing (along with some pointers from the pros).

Sporting clays

The farm offers two- and three-hour private and group courses for both novice and experienced clay shooters. Several courses are available including a skeet field, flurry field and four parcour stations.

drive

As you pull out of the gates of Blackberry Farm, you may feel like your weekend getaway can't go anywhere but down from here. But, you're headed to Asheville, home of the famed and luxurious Biltmore Estate. Located just 90 miles from Knoxville, the drive to Asheville is more scenic than the route from Nashville to Knoxville, with the Blue Ridge Mountains accompanying you along the way. Allow the folks at Blackberry Farm to pack up your gourmet lunch and hit the road. There's plenty awaiting you across the state line.

Departing Walland, take Highway 411 back to I-40 east toward Asheville. Journey through eastern Tennessee, up and over the beautiful Blue Ridge Mountain range (a perfect place to unwrap that gourmet grub to-go from Blackberry Farm), and continue over the state line and into North Carolina. When you arrive in the greater Asheville area, keep your eyes peeled for the I-240 exit taking you into downtown Asheville (www.exploreasheville.com).

stop

From farmers' markets to contemporary art galleries, Asheville is a hip and lively city center offering a diverse selection of things to do. First things first: Ditch the car. The best way to explore downtown Asheville is on foot, so select a parking spot or garage that is centrally located and plan to walk around the city. Galleries, independent shops and restaurants are abundant throughout the downtown center, so you should have no problem keeping yourself busy for the afternoon. Take a break from shopping to explore and

Scenes from Blackberry Farm

admire the architecture—you'll be surprised to find that many of the Art Deco buildings here rival what you might see in Miami Beach. After you've had your fill of downtown, begin to think about the main attraction and perhaps what put Asheville on the map in the first place: The Vanderbilt-commissioned Biltmore Estate. And you thought your weekend peaked back in Walland.

stay

★★★★Inn at Biltmore Estate

1 Antler Hill Road, Asheville, 800-411-3812, 828-255-1600; www.biltmore.com

The Biltmore Estate is, quite simply, beyond compare. Built in the late 1800s by George Vanderbilt, this castle set into the rolling landscape of the Blue Ridge Mountains is America's largest, and grandest, private home. The Inn on Biltmore Estate is a charming hideaway with luxurious accommodations, fine dining and a host of exciting outdoor pursuits. It's a perfect place for history buffs who want to re-live the refinement of a bygone era, and its location right on the estate grounds is unique. Hiking, horseback riding, biking and horse-drawn carriage rides provide a variety of ways to see the historic estate from different perspectives. Or, enjoy the view from a raft as you wind your way along the French Broad River, which cuts through the estate. Anglers will want to try their hand at fly-fishing on the lagoon, at

BLACKBERRY FARM

the property's fly-fishing school. The majestic Blue Ridge Mountains provide the backdrop for swimming or relaxing with a view at the inn's rimless, round pool. For the ultimate in luxury, reserve a night in the fully restored and elegant Biltmore Cottage. This two-bedroom cottage comes complete with its own personal butler and chef to provide you with plenty of pampering. 213 rooms. Wireless Internet access. Restaurant, bar. Airport transportation available. Fitness center. Pool. Spa. Business center. $$$

★★★★Richmond Hill Inn
87 Richmond Hill Drive, Asheville, 828-252-7313, 800-545-9338;
www.richmondhillinn.com

Richmond Hill provides a historic mansion setting, built in 1889 by 19th-century ambassador and Congressman Richmond Pearson and his wife, Gabrielle. Designer James G. Hill, a supervising architect for the U.S. Treasury buildings, created a structure that was artistic, innovative and ahead of its time with conveniences such as running water, a pulley-operated elevator for moving luggage, and a communications system. Located in the Blue Ridge Mountains not far from downtown Asheville, the mansion was a social hotspot for decades, but fell into disrepair in the 1950s. A $3 million restoration refurbished the mansion and it reopened in 1989 to house a combined 37 rooms, croquet cottages and a garden pavilion. The grand lobby is warm and inviting with high ceilings and walls covered with natural, amber-hued oak. The interiors feature upholstered drapery and numerous antiques, while the main staircase, leading from the lobby to the upstairs guest rooms, has wooden banisters and steps partially covered in a deep gold-patterned carpet. The well-kept grounds and gardens surround the small property with featured flowers and labeled trees. A "mountain brook" begins near the main house and ends at a 9-foot waterfall in the garden pavilion area as one of several water features on the property. The formal Parterre Garden is fashioned after Victorian-era gardens with simple, geometric shapes and pathways between flowerbeds. Guests play free on the croquet lawn with front-porch rockers overlooking the greens. Inside are fresh flowers on the mantel, chocolates on the pillow, magazines on the nightstand, a compact disc player with CDs, and soft drinks in the mini-fridge. Located three miles from downtown Asheville, the property is quiet and romantic.

37 rooms. Complimentary full breakfast. Wireless Internet access. Two restaurants, two bars. Fitness center. $$$

eat

★★★Gabrielle's

87 Richmond Hill Drive, Asheville, 828-252-7313, 800-545-9238; www.richmondhillinn.com

Victorian ambience and contemporary Southern cuisine fuse together at Gabrielle's within the Richmond Hill Inn. The restaurant includes two distinct areas: a large ballroom complete with rich, cherry-wood paneling, a three-tiered chandelier and period décor, and an enclosed sunroom that features views of the countryside, leather-wicker furniture and ceiling fans. Executive chef Duane Hernandes offers the choice between a seasonal three-course prix fixe and five-course chef's tasting menu. The prix fixe offers a choice of items such as fennel pollen-dusted wild Alaskan halibut and prosciutto di parma salad, while the chef's menu features more refined choices, including quail egg and sevruga caviar, chilled blue crab salad and toasted pistachio brûlée with chocolate sorbet to finish the meal.

American menu. Dinner. Bar. Business casual attire. Reservations recommended. Valet parking. $$$$

DOWNTOWN ASHEVILLE

★★★Flying Frog Café

1 Battery Park Ave., Asheville, 828-254-9411; www. flyingfrogcafe.com

The Flying Frog Restaurant is located in the the Haywood Park Hotel in the center of downtown Asheville. Decorated in an urban Indian theme, the restaurant features a dining area with half moon booths upholstered in a gold stripe fabric with multiple throw pillows. In another area of the dining room, Casablanca booths are draped with sheer curtains providing privacy. The restaurant also features a display kitchen and a private wine room. The variety of international menu options, from Indian bread platter to schnitzel, changes seasonally.

Continental, Indian, International menu. Dinner. Closed Monday-Tuesday. Bar. Business casual attire. Valet parking. $$$

TUPELO HONEY CAFE

★★★The Market Place Restaurant

20 Wall St., Asheville, 828-252-4162; www.marketplace-restaurant.com

Located on a side street in the center of downtown Asheville, in the vicinity of quaint shops, the Market Place features an eclectic décor and 5-foot brushed steel dividers—made by a local artist—between tables for privacy. The artist also created hammered copper folders to present the menus and billfolds. Rattan chairs are placed around the crisp set tables, and oil lamps, along with fresh flowers, add to the ambience. From the kitchen come organic cheeses and vegetables, free-range chickens, and local trout, among other locally grown and purveyed ingredients. Meat is smoked over hickory and oak. The recent addition of Bar 100 next door provides a casual dining option, or a place to enjoy a libation before dinner. American, French menu. Dinner. Closed Sunday. Bar. Casual attire. Outdoor seating. $$$

nn at Biltmore Estate • Conservatory Rose Garden • Biltmore Estate lagoon • Inn at Biltmore Estate

★★Tupelo Honey Café

12 College St., Asheville, 828-255-4404; www.tupelohoneycafe.com

Those looking for some good old Southern cookin' will find it at Tupelo Honey Café. Menu offerings range from fried green tomatoes to grit cakes to nutty fried chicken (and only free-range chicken at that). The décor is rather plain, with yellow walls, black-and-white photographs, storefront windows and exposed vent pipes, but snag a table on the sidewalk and Tupelo Honey serves as the perfect lunch perch. Or take a seat at the counter and watch chefs prepare the food at the exhibition kitchen. American menu. Breakfast, lunch, dinner, late-night. Closed Monday. Children's menu. Casual attire. Outdoor seating. $$

see

Biltmore Estate

1 Antler Hill Road, Asheville, 828-255-1333, 800-411-3812; www.biltmore.com

Whether you stay on the Biltmore property or not, a trip to the estate is a must when in Asheville. If you've got the whole day ahead of you, plan to start with breakfast at the inn. Large windows frame the view of the estate's grounds and make for the perfect morning wake-up call. From here, drive or take the hotel shuttle to the main house for a tour. Touted as America's largest private home and built in 1895, George Vanderbilt's 250-room mansion sits on more than 8,000 acres and is a stunning example of French Renaissance architecture. See priceless paintings and Napoleon's chess set. The interior of the estate features 65 fireplaces and a bowling alley. The estate's acres upon landscaped acres of gardens were originally the concept of famed landscape architect Frederick Law Olmsted (who designed New York's Central Park). With other activities including wine tasting at the estate's winery, equestrian activities, and the restored 19th-century River Bend Farm, Biltmore can easily consume an entire day. General tours of the mansion interior depart daily. (More extensive tours are available by reservation.)

BILTMORE ESTATE
SHRUB GARDEN

Biltmore Village

www.biltmorevillage.com
Located just outside the main gate of the estate, Biltmore Village was a community planned in the vision of George Vanderbilt. Today, the small shopping area offers an array of boutiques, galleries, restaurants and antique shops.

River Art District

The River Art District is home to dozens of working artist studios and local talents. With strong ties to the artist community, the River Art District is bursting with creativity including 30 art galleries such as the 14,000-square-foot **Blue Spiral 1** (*38 Biltmore Ave., 800-291-2513; www.bluespiral1.com*), showing the work of 38 artists, and **Overstrom Gallery** (*25 Wall St., 828-258-1761; www.overstrom.com*) featuring all handcrafted jewelry designs.

Woolworth Walk

25 Haywood St., Asheville, 828-254-9234;
www.woolworthwalk.com
While Woolworth is a thing of the past in most U.S. cities and a distant memory for current generations, it's still a thriving stop in Asheville. You'll want to explore Woolworth Walk downtown, especially if you're craving something sweet. Stop at the soda fountain for that perfect ice cream sundae or milkshake. Located in Asheville's original Woolworth 5 and 10 store, the soda fountain operates in the original location and still serves up fountain sodas, egg creams and shakes. The department store now houses Asheville's largest art gallery.

WINTER GARDEN AT
BILTMORE ESTATE

THE LAKE AT BILTMORE

drive

For the quickest trip back to Nashville (roughly five hours), take the same
drive back as you did on your trip up to Asheville, following signs for I-40
west. If you want to savor the Southern experience a bit longer, veer off on
the Blue Ridge Parkway, which joins up with Route 441 in Smoky Mountains National Park. Easily accessed just south of the Biltmore Estate, this
winding road will take you through both the Blue Ridge and Great Smoky
Mountain ranges. Because of the reduced speed limits and the nature of
this drive, it can add hours to the trip (and require an entire day of driving),
but if you've got the time, the views are spectacular.

CHAPTER 6
NEW YORK CITY TO NEWPORT

With so many places within driving distance of the Big Apple, New Yorkers often have a hard time choosing where to go for a long weekend. The three and a half hour trip from NYC to the seaside respite of Newport, Rhode Island not only ensures a magical final destination but also provides an opportunity to explore the many quaint Connecticut towns along the way, where you can shop, eat and stroll the quiet streets. By the time you get to gilded Newport, all the gridlock and noise of New York will feel as though it never existed. This picturesque island city is famous for its mansions, where America's elite used to summer, including the Vanderbilts, Astors and Kennedys. These lavish homes are well preserved, and in fact, the entire city still captures the splendor of that era, with its busy port lined with sailboats (a popular activity here) and charming streets full of great shopping and perfect little restaurants serving chowder and beers.

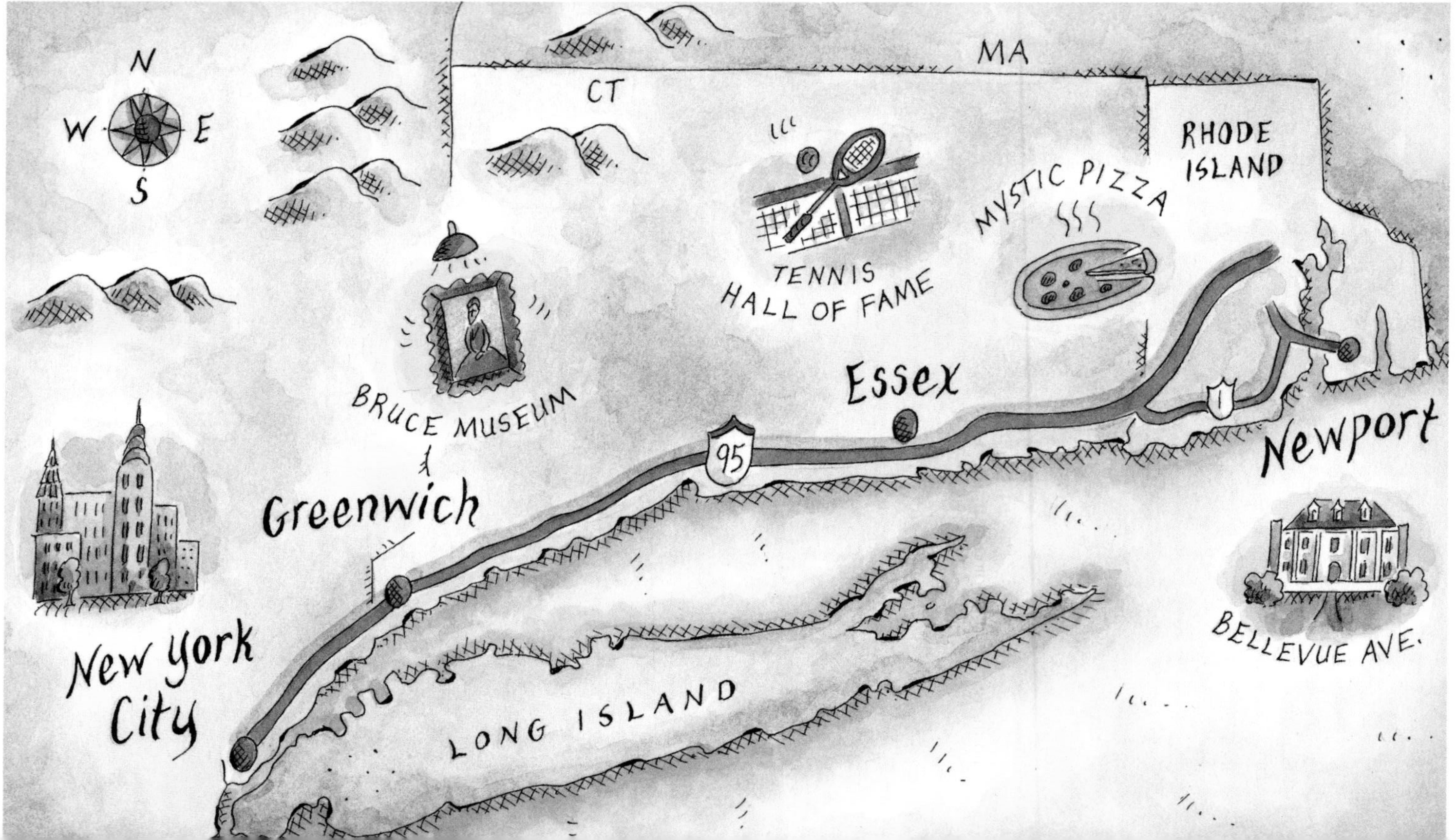

N
W · E
S

RHODE ISLAND

MA

CT

Newport

BELLEVUE AVE.

MYSTIC PIZZA $$$

TENNIS HALL OF FAME

Essex

95

LONG ISLAND

BRUCE MUSEUM

Greenwich

New York City

starting out

If you're spending a night or two in NYC, the Mobil Five-Star **Mandarin Oriental** (*80 Columbus Circle, New York, 212-805-8800, 866-801-8880; www. mandarinoriental.com/newyork*) is a serene and relaxing place occupying 54 floors of the Time Warner Center and offering spectacular views of Central Park, the Hudson River and the city skyline.

drive

After navigating the highway system surrounding New York City, you'll find that taxicabs and traffic lights give way to charming, tree-lined country roads leading to some of the most picturesque New England towns. Greenwich is about 30 minutes from New York and the trip is simple: Head north and east, following signs to Highway 678 north and then Interstate 95 north. You'll find winding highways leading from Manhattan through some of the wealthiest and well-known suburbs in the U.S. before arriving in the enchanting town of Greenwich. Because of Greenwich's close proximity to New York City, there aren't many desirable stops along the way. But once you reach Greenwich, there's plenty to do and see.

Brooklyn Bridge ▪ Mandarin Oriental▪ Manhattan ▪ A guest room at the Mandarin Oriental

stop

With a population surpassing 60,000 residents and a title as one of the most affluent communities in the U.S., the quiet Gotham suburb of Greenwich melds the sophistication of its high-end residents with the beauty of its agrarian past. Pristine lawns and plush mansions reside comfortably alongside quaint upscale boutiques and cozy downtown coffeehouses. From hidden beachfronts to sprawling meadows to yacht-filled harbors, Greenwich encompasses the elegance of luxury living while retaining a small-town appeal.

stay

★★★Homestead Inn

420 Field Point Road, Greenwich, 203-869-7500; www.homesteadinn.com
If the shopping of Greenwich is too much to tackle in one day, you're in luck: The historic luxury Homestead Inn, built in 1799, offers a secluded, romantic refuge in the heart of town. Purchased in 1997 and fully renovated

NEWPORT COASTLINE

by Thomas and Theresa Henkelmann, this historic New England inn now stands as a tribute to Theresa's interior decorating talents and Thomas's magnificent cooking (don't miss the Thomas Henkelmann restaurant just off the lobby). You'll find an eclectic mix of antique furniture, imported products, and one-of-a-kind touches on the ground floor and throughout the guest rooms and suites. It all amounts to a mix of imported pieces from India, China, Bali and Morocco, combined with solid cherry bespoke furniture, Frette linens, heated bathroom floors and original artwork. The inn also has a 24-hour concierge.

18 rooms. Closed two weeks in March. Children over 12 years only. Restaurant. Bar. $$$$

eat

★★★L'Escale Restaurant
500 Steamboat Road, Greenwich, 203-661-4600; www.lescalerestaurant.com
For the most festive lunch spot after a morning on the shopping circuit, walk or drive down Main Street to the Delamar Hotel and the adjacent restaurant L'Escale, which transports guests to a riverside bistro in the heart of France. Seaside seating on the dock is first come, first served, and provides the perfect lunch perch on a sunny day on Greenwich Harbor. The provincial menu—which changes daily—uses the freshest seafood and herbs to satisfy even the most discerning diner. Whether you fancy a lunch of steamed shellfish, beef carpaccio or provençal tarte, L'Escale offers fine food and an exceptional setting in which to enjoy it. Dinnertime is an elaborate affair at L'Escale, as the dining room is adorned with dozens of candles and fresh flowers, creating the ultimate in golden hues.
French, Mediterranean menu. Breakfast, lunch, dinner, Sunday brunch. Bar. Business casual attire. Reservations recommended. Valet parking. Outdoor seating. $$$

★★★Thomas Henkelmann
420 Field Point Road, Greenwich, 203-869-7500; www.homesteadinn.com
Located in the historic Homestead Inn, this fine dining restaurant featuring the cuisine of chef/owner and namesake Thomas Henkelmann provides

a cozy setting for enjoying inventive dishes based around seasonal ingredients. German- and Geneva-trained Henkelmann serves up multiple courses that rely on French influences—pâté of duck with truffles and pistachios, goat cheese beignet and oven baked loin of rabbit, to name a few. Enjoy the fine cuisine among the comforts of home as the dining rooms feature fireplaces, upholstered chairs, exposed beams and upscale country décor.

French menu. Breakfast, lunch, dinner. Closed Sunday; also two weeks in March. Bar. Jacket required. Reservations recommended. Valet parking. $$$$

shop

Main Street and Richard's of Greenwich

359 Greenwich Ave., Greenwich, 203-622-0551; www.mitchellsonline.com

While this wealthy bedroom community may seem greatly removed from the bustling island of Manhattan, it actually has a downtown shopping district that rivals New York's own Fifth Avenue, Chicago's Magnificent Mile and Beverly Hills' Rodeo Drive. From Tiffany to Ralph Lauren, Kate Spade to Saks Fifth Avenue, Greenwich's Main Street (Greenwich Ave.) is a virtual hopscotch of luxury brands. And you won't want to pass by local department store-turned-design mecca Richard's of Greenwich without a stop to peruse the latest from Prada, Burberry and Cartier. The newly expanded Westport-based retailer recently moved from its 9,000-square-foot home to a space three times the size across Main Street and is chockfull of high-end wearables. Monday-Wednesday, Friday 9:30 a.m.-6 p.m., Thursday 9:30 a.m.-8 p.m., Saturday 8:30 a.m.-9 p.m.

Aux Delices Foods by Debra Ponzek

3 W. Elm St., Greenwich, 203-622-6644; www.auxdelicesfoods.com

Serious shopping can stir up anyone's appetite and while there are plenty of casual dining options in and around the Main Street area, you may wish to recharge with a stop at Greenwich's own Aux Delices Foods by Debra Ponzek. The name translates to "all the wonderful things in life" and the menu lives up to its moniker: this charming little café and gourmet food to-go shop is the perfect retreat for grabbing a cool beverage and bakery treat to match, or a selection from the ever-changing breakfast menu of morning delectables.

WINE BAR AT THE GRISWOLD INN

A SAILBOAT PASSING CASTLE HILL INN

see
Bruce Museum of Arts and Science
1 Museum Drive, Greenwich, 203-869-6786; www.brucemuseum.org
Once the private home of textile merchant Robert Moffat Bruce, the structure now houses an art and science museum in his name and hosts permanent exhibitions as well as changing exhibits, often centering around a local focus. From archaeology digs to Paris portraits, the Bruce museum spans many different interests and time periods. Tuesday-Saturday 10 a.m.-5 p.m., Sunday 1-5 p.m., closed Monday.

drive
After a leisurely evening spent dining and unwinding in Greenwich, continue east along I-95 and follow signs for New Haven. If you find yourself getting antsy by the time you hit Stamford, take exit 12 (15 minutes past Stamford) for a jaunt through the pleasant seaside town of Rowayton.

stop
This charming coastal town is known for its stunning marshes and active harbor filled with sailboats. And for a town so small, Rowayton certainly knows its food. Try to time your trip so that you're here for lunch. **The Restaurant at Rowayton Seafood** (*89 Rowayton Ave., 203-866-4488; www.rowaytonseafood.com*), referred to as "The Restaurant" by locals, is one of Connecticut's only waterfront restaurants open year-round. Enjoy a dockside hand-picked Maine lobster roll and selection from the ample wine list. Or, head down the street to the local favorite **River Cat Grill** (*148 Rowayton Ave., 203-854-0860; www.rivercatgrill.com*) for a signature order of lobster mac' n' cheese. Before leaving town, be sure to check out

the **Rowayton Country Market** (*157 Rowayton Ave., 203-852-0011*) to stock up on sundries for your drive up the coast.

drive
Continue east on I-95 to New Haven, where you will see signs for Route 1, the famous Post Road (originally Boston Post Road, established way back in the late 17th century) that veers away from I-95 just east of New Haven and supplies a more picturesque journey along the coastline. History buffs can relish in knowing that this same Post Road was traveled by Benjamin Franklin and Paul Revere and once served as the only route between New York and Boston.

stop
Just over an hour outside New Haven on Route 1, turn left at Route 9 north and follow it until you reach the sleepy town of Essex (*www.essexct.com*), the self-proclaimed "best small town in America." Drive down Main Street and peruse the high-end boutiques and antiques shops housed in traditional New England-style buildings, some with wooden shutters and weathered shingles. If you're looking for a wearable souvenir, head straight to **J. Alden Clothiers** (*17 Main St., Essex, 877-952-5336; www.jaldenclothiers.com*), where you can score nautical-inspired ties, belts and bags, as well as luxe cashmere apparel and Audrey Talbott designs. Be sure to venture over to the **Griswold Inn** (*36 Main St., 860-767-1776; www.griswoldinn.com*). "The Gris" may not be known for luxury, but as one of the oldest continually operating inns in the country, this colonial building from 1776 is worth a stop. Pull up a chair in one of the five unique dining

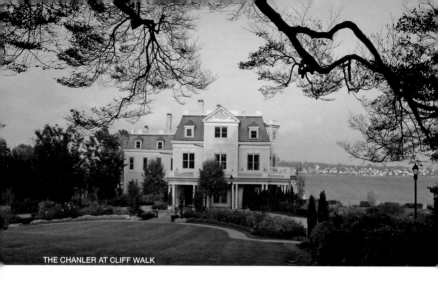
THE CHANLER AT CLIFF WALK

rooms for a bowl of creamy New England clam chowder, before strolling down to the docks to discover the waterfront **Connecticut River Museum** (*67 Main St., 860-767-8269; www.ctrivermuseum.org*), where one can experience the wonders of New England's Great River.

drive

From Essex, an easy 15-minute drive south on Highway 154 will bring you to Old Saybrook, another quaint seaside community. One of the oldest towns in the state (1854), and the oldest on the Connecticut shoreline, Old Saybrook offers beautiful shores, vistas, marinas and an eclectic collection of shops and restaurants on its charming Main Street. If you didn't grab a bite before, stop off at the Mobil Three-Star **Saybrook Point Inn & Spa** (*2 Bridge St., 800-243-0212; www.saybrook.com*) where warm upscale interiors and courteous service define a luxury seaside getaway. Located on Saybrook Point and surrounded by water on three sides, the location is perfect for views of Long Island Sound and the Connecticut River—one of New England's most precious scenic backdrops. The restaurant, **Terra Mar**, serves the best lobster rolls in town.

stop

After you've sufficiently stretched your legs, hop back in the car and continue east on Route 1. Enjoy photo-opp vistas from the driver's seat as the road weaves up the coast and merges onto Highway 138 E, taking you over the Jamestown and Claiborne Pell bridges toward scenic Newport.

The famous mansions lining the streets with their backyards facing the sea are some of the most impressive homes anywhere, even in the modern age, making it hard to believe they were only vacation homes in their earlier heyday. Bellevue Avenue, the main drag and home to many of the famed mansions, is a tourist destination in all seasons, but especially during the summer. Many of the houses now stand as national historic landmarks including Marble House, Rosecliff and The Breakers. Originally built for William Vanderbilt's older brother, Cornelius II, The Breakers, at 44 Ochre Point Ave., stands a 70-room Italian-style "palazzo" made to mirror Italian palaces. The intricate and lavish interior was no afterthought; relief sculptures and muraled ceilings are just a few features of the breathtaking design.

You will certainly want to explore the rich history of the luxury cottages here, as well as the lives of the people who resided in them. But the houses are only half the attraction: The views of Narragansett Bay and Newport Harbor are likely what brought such fame and fortune to Newport in the first place. Reserve time during your visit for a scenic drive along the coast—and aim to get there before sunset. If you have only moments to spare before the sun goes down, head for the beach between Newport and Middleton and use your car as a perch to watch joggers, dog-walkers and people frolic along the sand. If you have a bit more time and are game for some exercise after being cooped up in the car all afternoon, park your car an hour or two before sunset and navigate the 3.5-mile Cliff Walk—a path from which you'll be treated to spectacular sunset views.

Guest room at The Chanler at Cliff Walk • The Chanler at Cliff Walk • Guest room at Castle Hill Inn • Castle Hill Inn

stay

★★★The Chanler at Cliff Walk

117 Memorial Boulevard, Newport, 401-847-1300; www.thechanler.com
Retire for the night in one of 20 rooms at this mansion-turned-hotel. Each of Chanler's rooms is uniquely designed to represent a different historical period or theme and its Ocean Villas are particularly luxurious with their own private water views, saunas and whirlpools. Manicured grounds, gardens and antique paintings epitomize Newport's regal charm, while guest rooms award travelers with thoughtful amenities including DVD players, fireplaces and marble and granite bathrooms with heated floors, multiple showerheads and jetted tubs. If you're feeling particularly indulgent, request a butler-drawn bath or in-room massage treatment. After a peaceful night's sleep, enjoy a complimentary breakfast in the Spiced Pear restaurant, once again taking advantage of the view from the terrace overlooking Amagansett Bay and Cliff Walk.
20 Rooms. Wireless Internet access. Restaurant. Bar. $$$$

eat

★★★Castle Hill Inn & Resort

590 Ocean Drive, Newport, 401-849-3800, 888-466-1355; www.castlehillinn.com

Boasting another spectacular sunset vista, the Castle Hill Inn is the perfect place to stop for an early evening cocktail. The impressive arched wall of windows at the inn's restaurant provides spectacular 180-degree Narragansett Bay views and sunset panoramas on clear evenings. After a few glasses of bubbly, treat your palate to one of the chef's thoughtful tasting menus or a variety of à la carte dishes. Indulge your tastebuds in chilled Sakonnet River oysters paired with a saffron sorbet or try Elysian Fields lamb rack with braised greens and a ricotta-spring garlic ravioli. And if the thought of staying in an historic 1874 mansion is too much to pass up, stay the night (no children are allowed in mansion accommodations). An adjacent chalet, the Harbor House, and beach houses and cottages are the epitome of elegance and romance.

35 rooms. Complimentary full breakfast. Wireless Internet access. Restaurant, two bars. Beach. Airport transportation available. Business center. $$$$

FLUKE WINE BAR & KITCHEN

Spiced Pear Restaurant

117 Memorial Blvd., Newport, 401-847-2244; www.spicedpear.com

With stellar views and fine cuisine, the Spiced Pear serves lunch on its cliffside veranda and offers succulent treats, including Kobe beef ribs and an organic salad of beets. For dinner, choose between an à la carte menu and the chef's eight-course tasting feast. With tables that will remind you of the lavish living and dining rooms of the nearby mansions, you'll want to reserve a good chunk of time for dinner here. If you decide to stop by the restaurant on your way out of town, Spiced Pear also serves a full Sunday brunch menu from 11:30 a.m.-2:30 p.m.

American menu. Breakfast, lunch, dinner, Sunday brunch. Outside seating. $$$$

Fluke Wine Bar & Kitchen

41 Bowens Wharf, Newport, 401-849-7778; www.flukewinebar.com

After a day of driving, head to the piers in downtown Newport and look for the unsuspecting Fluke Wine Bar, which seems to appear out of nowhere on Bowens Wharf. Sample one of the many wines by the glass and nibble on seafood-heavy small

NEWPORT HARBOR

MARBLE HOUSE

plates including lobster salad sliders (a house favorite), PEI mussels and marcona almond-stuffed dates.

Continental menu. Dinner, Sunday brunch. $$$

see

International Tennis Hall of Fame

194 Bellevue Ave., Newport, 401-849-3990; www.tennisfame.com

If mansion-viewing gets tiresome, grab a racket and head to the courts at the International Tennis Hall of Fame. You can actually reserve court time and play on the same grass courts that hosted tennis greats such as Billie Jean King, Martina Navratilova, John McEnroe, Chris Evert and John Newcombe. The site itself is significant for hosting the first-ever U.S. National Championships in 1881. Inside the Hall of Fame Museum, test your knowledge of the game and relive the sport's past through memorabilia, videos and interactive exhibits. $10 admission. Daily 9:30 a.m.-5 p.m.

Cliff Walk

Memorial Blvd. (parking at Easton's Beach); www.cliffwalk.com

This scenic walking path features peerless views incorporating the man-made beauty of Newport's elegant homes and the natural vista of the New England coastline and lush green shore. Beginning at Memorial Boulevard, the trail blends pavement, gravel and sea rock, and reigns as the best spot in Newport to watch the sun set into the sea as the waves crash on one side of the path and the enormous back yards of Newport's historic mansions rest on the other. Be sure to traverse the 40 steps, a dramatic stone stairwell that drops about two thirds of the way down the cliff to a balcony overlooking the sea. During Newport's golden age, these steps were a gathering place for servants and maids from the nearby mansions.

Fort Adams

1 Lincoln Drive, 401-841-0707; www.fortadams.org
Newport's pristine waterfront setting proves a great
site to catch some rays or set sail. But its coastal
location also served as a military defense throughout American history. From 1854 to 1950, Fort Adams, located just across Newport Harbor, served
as a barracks for U.S. soldiers. Today, it stands as
the largest coastal fort in the country. A short water
taxi ride from the mainland allows visitors access
to guided fort tours including officers' quarters,
casemates, parade field, a listening tunnel and
a climb up to a scenic overlook with spectacular
view of the harbor and beyond to Narragansett
Bay. $10 admission. Mid-May to October,
10 a.m.-4 p.m.

Newport Mansions Experience

*The Preservation Society of Newport County, 424 Bel-
levue Ave., 401-847-1000; www.newportmansions.org*
While you can comfortably tour Newport's famed
homes from your car or on foot from the outside,
some mansions are also open to the public for
interior tours. And though many properties are still
privately owned and maintained, the Preservation
Society of Newport County currently manages 11
properties, including the Breakers, The Elms and
Chateau-sur-Mer. Learn how Cornelius Vanderbilt's grandson's summer "cottage" acquired the
name Marble House. (Hint: 500,000 cubic feet of
marble, reportedly costing $7 million at the time
it was built in the early 1890s, were used in its
construction.) Or explore the exquisite gardens and
grand ballrooms of another Newport masterpiece,
Rosecliff *(548 Bellevue Ave.),* which was commissioned in 1899 by silver heiress Tessie Oelrichs
with the purpose of hosting elaborate parties and
gatherings. There are a variety of tour packages
to choose from, ranging from entry into any five
of the 11 mansions to after-hours tours of The
Elms. No visit to Newport is complete until you're
past the wrought-iron gates and gazing into room
after room of exquisite wallpaper, lavish décor and
priceless antique furniture.

FORT ADAMS

DINING ROOM AT MARBLE
HOUSE

DINING ROOM AT CASTLE HILL INN

drive

On the way out of Newport, as you bid the sweeping lawns and mansions farewell, stop for a quick hot beverage at **Empire Tea & Coffee** (*22 Broadway, 401-619-1388; Monday-Friday 7 a.m.-10 p.m., Saturday-Sunday 9 a.m.-10 p.m.*). A charming yet bare-bones coffee and tea shop, Empire features more than 60 varieties of gourmet loose teas as well as a host of other hot and cold drinks. Try the frozen hot chocolate on a warm day or a chai noir (chai tea with chocolate) if you find yourself in Newport during the winter.

Head out of town via Ocean Drive for one of the most scenic and breathtaking drives on the eastern seaboard. The drive combines a glimpse of the rich history of the wealthy summer community with miles and miles of public access shoreline and stunning homes seen from afar. You'll pass by boulders, sheep, creeks and little inlets as you head back toward Route 1. Before leaving the small, charming towns of Rhode Island and Connecticut, make time for a slice of pizza in Mystic.

eat

★Mystic Pizza
56 West Main St., Mystic, 860-536-3700; www.mysticpizza.com
This pizza place put the tiny town of Mystic, Connecticut on the map. Mystic Pizza opened in 1973 and served as the site of Julia Roberts' big screen career breakthrough 15 years later (in the film, *Mystic Pizza*) Today, the restaurant (which has since opened a second location, Mystic Pizza II) still serves the same big "slices of heaven" it did 30 years ago, and has maintained its local appeal.
Pizza menu. Lunch, dinner. $

drive

With a fountain soda in the cup holder and a belly full of cheese, it's officially time to hightail it back to the big city. Head west on West Main Street (Route 1) and make a right on Allyn Street. Allyn becomes Mystic Street and after just over a mile will merge onto I-95 South. As small towns make way for highways and highrises, follow signs on I-95 directing you back to New York City. Back in the city limits and with all the modern-day conveniences of an urban mecca, you may find yourself missing the gems of New England's tiny towns and quiet sidewalks. Rest assured; another New England adventure remains only a few hours away.

CHAPTER 7
SAN DIEGO TO LAGUNA BEACH

There's a good reason for the constant flow of people to and from California's coastal points: The southern California coast offers spectacular views throughout the year, as well as fantastic dining and lodging options to accompany the scenery. Make the hour-and-a-half trip up the coast from laid-back San Diego to Laguna Beach for a luxurious weekend getaway. You'll see why everyone from surf bums to some of the wealthiest individuals in the country call this region home. Few places offer such a breadth of cultural and natural landscapes, from the Pacific-swept beaches to the cliffs and canyons of the San Joaquin Hills, amidst such luxurious accommodations. Like its coastal sisters, Laguna has all the allure of a beachside city but has a distinct personality of its own with its a hilly landscape, artsy twist and decidedly friendly atmosphere. If you were a fan of the TV show *The O.C.*, pile in the car and start singing..."We've been on the run, driving in the sun, looking out for number one, California here we come!"

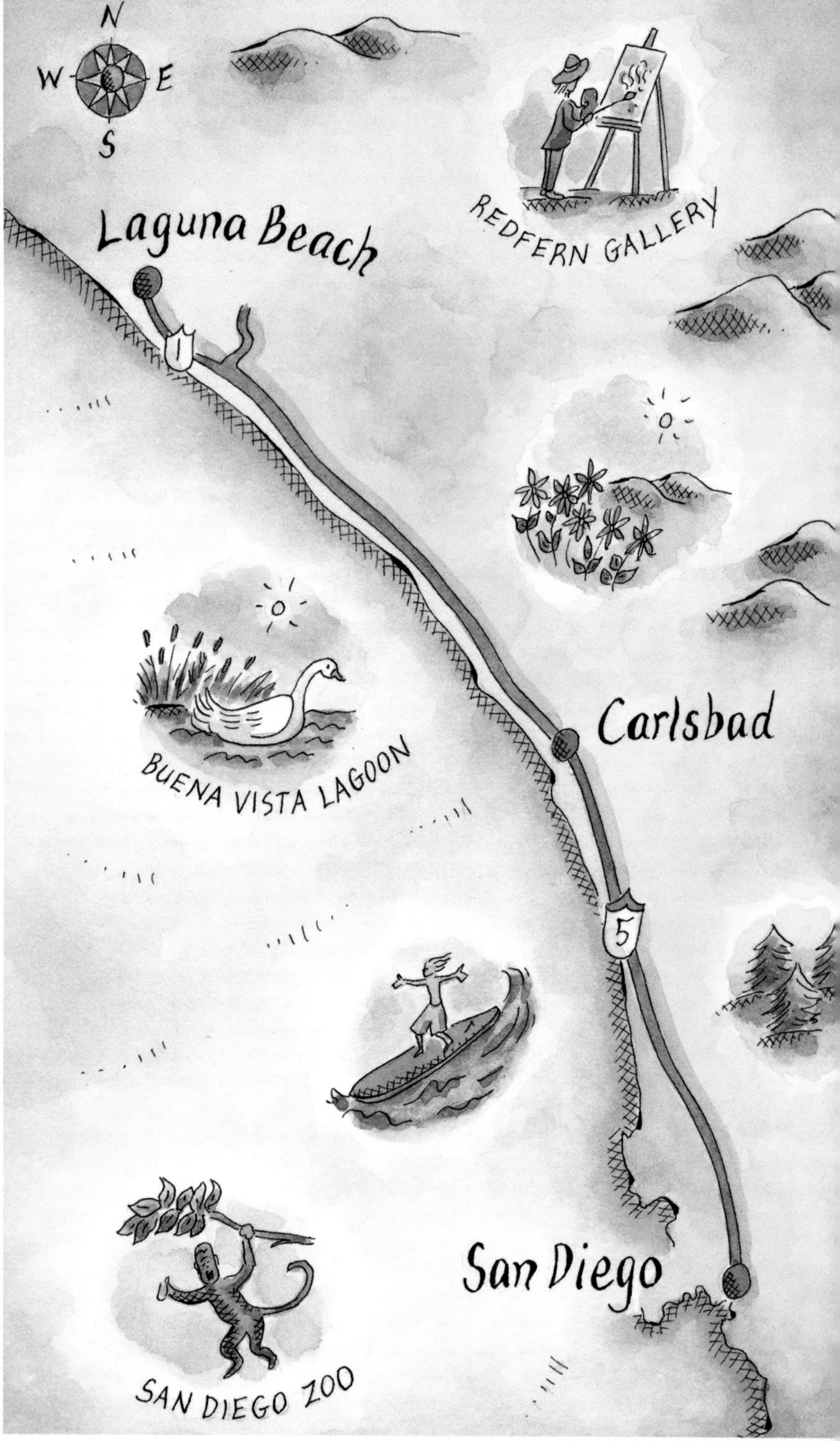

N
W
E
S
Laguna Beach
REDFERN GALLERY
1
Carlsbad
BUENA VISTA LAGOON
5
San Diego
SAN DIEGO ZOO

LAGUNA BEACH

starting out

Spend a night or two in San Diego at the Mobil Four-Star **U.S. Grant Hotel**
(*326 Broadway, San Diego, 866-837-4270, 800-237-5029; www.usgrant.net*).
This nearly 100-year hotel, which was opened in 1910 by Ulysses S. Grant,
Jr. and his wife Francine, recently underwent a multi-million dollar renova-
tion that restored the polish to the historic, grand building.

drive

As you head north on Interstate 5 from San Diego, you'll reach the small
seaside city of Carlsbad in about 30 minutes. The trip is all on the highway,
but the vistas from I-5 are more scenic than most with the Pacific on your
left and the ritzy communities of La Jolla and Del Mar along the way. After
you pass Encinitas, keep your eyes out for signs for exit 50 to Carlsbad.
This beach-oriented community is a virtual playground for golfers, tennis
players, water skiers, fishing enthusiasts and luxury road-trippers. In addition to the Carlsbad Skatepark, a popular destination for locals of all ages,
and the Buena Vista Lagoon, Carlsbad hosts a spectacular field of flowers
that is revered throughout the state. In peak season (May), the commercial flower fields invite visitors to marvel at Mother Nature's kaleidoscope
of colors. Take the Palomar Airport Road exit to visit the Flower Fields at
Carlsbad Ranch—and don't forget your camera.

stay

★★★★Four Seasons Resort Aviara, North San Diego

*7100 Four Seasons Point, Carlsbad, 760-603-6800, 800-819-5053;
www.fourseasons.com/aviara*

Avid golfers come to play the 18-hole golf course designed by Arnold
Palmer. But that's just one reason to come to this splendid resort on 200
lush acres overlooking the Batiquitos Lagoon, the Pacific Ocean and a
nature preserve that's home to a variety of wildlife. The architecture pays
homage to the region's history with its Spanish colonial design, and guest
rooms feel luxurious and homey, with sumptuous sitting areas, sliding
French doors that open up to private patios or balconies, and marble bath-

ST. REGIS RESORT,
MONARCH BEACH

POOL AT ST. REGIS RESORT,
MONARCH BEACH

rooms with deep soaking tubs. Dining choices range from Italian to California cuisine and the lively wine bar boasts dramatic floor-to-ceiling windows offering views of the Pacific.

318 rooms. Two restaurants, bar. Children's activity center. Fitness center. Spa. Pool. Golf. Tennis. Business center. Pets accepted. $$$$

eat

★★★Vivace

7100 Four Seasons Point, Carlsbad, 760-603-6999;
www.fourseasons.com/aviara/dining

While you can venture into neighboring towns for dining options around Carlsbad, you really don't have to look beyond this restaurant at the Four Seasons. Tuscan inspiration permeates the dining room and adjoining terrace. A large light stone fireplace fills the dining room with warmth, intimacy and romance, while the floor-to-ceiling windows allow breathtaking views of the ocean and lagoon—all reinforcing the casual sophistication of the restaurant and its menu. A central Italian influence resonates within the menu, from the antipasti to the entrées. Antipasti present a multitude of light fare options, including tuna crudo with red onion marjoram aïoli. There is also a vast selection of pastas, but with their own Vivace influence: black spaghetti with rock shrimp and calabrese sausage; hand-made orecchiette with braised capon; and "spaghetti di verdure" with chanterelles, spring onions and thin asparagus.

Italian menu. Dinner. Bar. Business casual attire. Reservations recommended. Valet parking. Outdoor seating. $$$

see

Flower Fields at Carlsbad Ranch

5704 Paseo Del Norte, Carlsbad, 760-431-0352;
www.theflowerfields.com

From its roots as a family-owned flower operation, the annual Flower Fields at Carlsbad Ranch have bloomed into a local phenomenon, thanks to the beautiful Tecolote Ranunculus. In certain sections, the field becomes a surreal sea of golds, pinks and purples from the sheer mass of the blooms. A British immigrant and horticulturist brought this Asian relative of the buttercup to California, where it now grows on 50 acres. Locals consider the March flowering to be a harbinger of spring, and more than 150,000 visitors come annually to check it out. Open daily from March to May.

The Village

Downtown Carlsbad, otherwise known as The Village, is home to an array of restaurants and shops, including antique shops, as well as a popular farmers' market on Saturday mornings (9 a.m.-1 p.m.). Explore the other areas in Carlsbad and you'll find many planned housing developments and the exclusive Southwest Quadrant where large and beautiful homes rest along a backdrop of rolling California hills.

drive

Departing from your oceanside perch in Carlsbad and continuing north along the winding I-5, you'll drive past the vast Camp Pendleton Marine Corps Base in your approach to southern Orange County. The 125,000-acre base, the largest expeditionary training facility on the West Coast, and the area surrounding it are home to thousands of active-duty and retired U.S. marines.

Vivace restaurant • Views of the St. Regis Resort, Monarch Beach

As you cruise past the halfway point between San Diego and Los Angeles, you'll approach your final destination. Recently made famous by many television shows and namesake of the MTV series set here, you may recognize the gorgeous beaches and monstrous homes of Laguna Beach and bordering Dana Point. Travel first through Dana Point, a small city just south of Laguna. Dana Point boasts its own beach as well as one of Orange County's most elegant resorts, the St. Regis Resort, Monarch Beach. Even from I-5, you can see the ocean peek out from the distance like a blue ribbon along the horizon. I-5 will take you to Highway 1 (the drive from Carlsbad will take just under an hour) at Capistrano Beach for the most scenic approach to Laguna Beach. If you have time, it's worth a visit to the St. Regis. Even if you're not staying the night, munch on an appetizer at the lobby terrace, which overlooks an azure ocean below.

If you haven't had enough of the Pacific Ocean, continue north on Highway 1 until you reach Laguna Beach, where you will notice that the sea meets colorful homes stacked along its high hills.

VERANDA AT THE RITZ-CARLTON, LAGUNA NIGUEL

stop

With few roads granting access to this idyllic town because of its mountainous topography and surrounding parkland, Laguna has a distinctly different feel than nearby Newport, which sports a stylish, affluent air; instead, Laguna is more often recognized for its arty influence, bungalow-style homes fringing the hilltops and, of course, as home to the best beaches along Orange County's coast.

Thought to be originally named Lagunas for Spanish "lagoons," freshwater lakes and canyons that occupied the area, Laguna Beach has forever been an alluring retreat for celebrities, artists, and even presidents—President Nixon only lived a few miles down the coast. Today, this charming seaside community offers a little bit of paradise for every appetite, from whale watching and art festivals to wine tasting and antique galleries. Or, you can simply come for the view.

Upon arriving, look out for the statue of Eiler Larsen, who was known as Laguna Beach's famed "greeter." The Denmark native moved to the town in the early 1930s and soon took to his role as greeter to everyone—tourists and residents alike—who visited the coastal town with an amiable "Hello, there!" Though he earned a living as a gardener, his hobby as the town greeter (officially recognized by the Laguna Beach city council) made Laguna Beach all the more warm-welcoming. One of Larsen's humble statues stands in front of the **Pottery Shack** (*1492 South Coast Highway*), adjacent to **Sapphire Restaurant** (*1212 South Coast Highway*), so be sure to take a peek.

stay

★★★★Montage Laguna Beach
30801 S. Coast Highway, Laguna Beach, 949-715-6000, 866-271-6953;
www.montagelagunabeach.com

Reigning over Laguna Beach from its rugged clifftop location, this stylish getaway blends arts and crafts style with the luxury of a full-service resort. Rooms, suites and bungalows feature 400-thread-count linens and marble bathrooms with a large shower and tub, and private balconies or patios with ocean views. Dining at Montage takes sophisticated California cuisine to a new level, particularly at the romantically cozy oceanfront bungalow restaurant, Studio. The full-range spa has more than 20 treatment rooms and the poolside cabanas are decked out with flat-screen TVs and DVD/CD players.

250 rooms. Wireless Internet access. Three restaurants, four bars. Fitness center. Pool. Beach. Pets accepted. $$$$

Montage Laguna Beach coastlilne ▪ Montage balcony views ▪ Studio restaurant ▪ Cabanas at the Montage

★★★★The Ritz-Carlton, Laguna Niguel

1 Ritz-Carlton Drive, Dana Point, 949-240-2000, 800-241-3333; www.ritzcarlton.com

Situated atop a 150-foot bluff overlooking the ocean, this Mediterranean style villa is a first-class haven. Guest rooms have been decorated in a palette of cream and soft blue to reflect the beach setting and have ocean, pool or garden views. The resort has three restaurants, including the unique wine tasting room ENO, which offers an extensive menu of wines, cheeses and chocolates from around the globe. Surfing lessons are available at the beach, and the spa is fabulous with its contemporary California-glam décor and full menu of luxe treatments. Golfers come to play several spectacular courses nearby.

393 rooms. Wireless Internet access. Three restaurants, bar. Fitness center. Pool. Tennis. Business center. Pets accepted. $$$$

★★★★★St. Regis Resort, Monarch Beach

1 Monarch Beach Resort, Dana Point, 949-234-3200; www.stregismb.com

Even seasoned travelers will swoon over the luscious, secluded setting and the Tuscan-inspired design of this resort, which is tucked away on 200 acres high above the Pacific Ocean. Elegant marble floors, plush carpets and massive sofas grace the public areas. The oversized guest rooms have dramatic contemporary décor with wood shutters, marble bathrooms, private balconies, goose down comforters and 300-thread count sheets. The resort has an 18-hole championship golf course, award-winning spa, beach club (with surfing lessons) and nature trails. In between, dine at one of the six ocean-view restaurants.

400 rooms. High-speed Internet access. Six restaurants, three bars. Fitness center. Spa. Beach. Pool. Golf. Tennis. Business center. Pets accepted. $$$$

STONEHILL TAVERN

eat

★★★★Stonehill Tavern

1 Monarch Beach Resort, Dana Point, 949-234-3318;
www.michaelmina.net/stonehill

Famed San Francisco chef-turned-restaurateur Michael Mina's urban bistro, located in the St. Regis, is a sleek, intimate spot designed by Tony Chi with comfortable couches, glass-enclosed booths and a large terrace. The menu includes Mina's signature appetizer trios—three different preparations of one ingredient, such as tuna, lobster or duck, as well as twists on American classics (think fried chicken with mascarpone polenta and a root beer float for dessert). An impressive wine program focuses on boutique California producers, but also includes a diverse selection from Austria and Burgundy.

American menu. Dinner. Closed Monday-Tuesday. Bar. Business casual attire. Reservations recommended. Valet parking. Outdoor seating. $$$$

★★★★Studio

30801 S. Coast Highway, Laguna Beach, 949-715-6420;
www.studiolagunabeach.com

Housed in a cozy arts and crafts cottage overlooking the ocean, this restaurant at Montage Laguna Beach is a study in understated elegance. The menu is the creation of award-winning chef James Boyce and features contemporary California cuisine made with the freshest local ingredients. Settle in for a supper made up of dishes like pan-seared John Dory with baby fennel, cipollini onions and caramelized cauliflower, or vinegar-braised short ribs with butter-roasted asparagus. The wine cellar features more than 1,800 bottles with plenty of California selections and wines available by the glass.

California menu. Dinner. Closed Monday. $$$

Sapphire

1200 S. Coast Highway, Laguna Beach, 949-715-9888; www.sapphirellc.com

Certainly a jewel by the sea, Sapphire restaurant's outdoor patio seating gives a perfect opportunity to savor the sparkling sea and its delicious California cuisine at the same time. Order the salmon served with a pineapple, mango and cilantro relish that adds a welcome acidity to the richness of the fish. There is also the Cobb salad, which resembles nothing like a conventional Cobb but excellent nonetheless with thin slices of shrimp and lobster nestled on a bed of nutty, baby field greens. California menu. Lunch, dinner, Saturday-Sunday brunch. Casual attire. Reservations recommended. Outdoor seating. $$

SPA MONTAGE

spa

★★★★★Spa Montage at Montage Laguna Beach

30801 S. Coast Highway, Laguna Beach, 949-715-6000, 866-271-6953; www.spamontage.com

Spa Montage is a stunning facility that takes advantage of its superior beachfront setting. An indoor-outdoor structure and floor-to-ceiling windows framing 160-degree views alleviate any guilt guests may feel for opting to stay in for a bit of pampering on a sunny day. The spa's holistic, get-back-to-nature approach is evident in its design, as well as in the products it uses. Custom-mixed lotions and oils blend natural ingredients, including eucalyptus, lavender, orange blossoms and citrus. Wrap up in one of the spa's plush robes and try any number of therapies, from a California citrus polish to an algae cellulite massage. Hungry spa-goers can find a cozy spot by the lap pool, where healthy snacks and meals are available from the Mosaic Grille.

★★★★The Ritz-Carlton Spa, Laguna Niguel

1 Ritz-Carlton Drive, Dana Point, 949-240-2000, 800-241-3333; www.ritzcarlton.com

It might seem hard to imagine driving all this way to spend the afternoon in your hotel, but one look at this state-of-the-art spa, and you'll understand. Eleven treatment rooms, a full service beauty salon, a circular manicure and pedicure station and a modern fitness center are available to guests at the Ritz-Carlton Spa. Choose from holistic treatments

SPA GAUGIN

that incorporate ancient practices as well as the latest skin treatments, massages and exfoliations. Collagen infusion facials and California citrus body polishes stand out among the spa's signature treatments. There are also seasonal treatments such as a summer chocolate sugar scrub pedicure. Treatments are rooted in the sea's purifying elements: rich minerals, sea salt or nutrient-rich algae and water.

★★★★Spa Gaucin
1 Monarch Beach Resort, Dana Point, 949-234-3367, 800-722-1543; www.stregismonarchbeach.com
Spa Gaucin at the St. Regis is the picture of elegance with dark woods, Asian-style accents and three-story waterfalls. The warm cream interior accentuates specially commissioned artwork throughout the space and the 25 treatment rooms offer state-of-the-art amenities (including gas fireplaces to cozy up to). The spa menu includes everything from Mediterranean massage to total vitamin facials to the Chardonnay sugar scrub. Try the Solace Mineral Trio, a hydrating treatment utilizing grapeseed body exfoliation and a volcanic clay wrap, or the Dermal Quench facial to ward off road-lag. There's also an extensive offering of beauty treatments from microdermabrasion to pedicures.

see
Laguna Art Museum
307 Cliff Drive, Laguna Beach, 949-494-8971; www.lagunaartmuseum.org
Artists have flocked to Laguna since the 1800s for inspiration, and there remains no better place to see the fruits of their labor than the Laguna Art Museum. With perhaps the largest permanent collection of artwork by Californian artists and ever-

changing exhibitions, this museum is a great option for those looking to experience Laguna's early days. Daily 11 a.m.-5 p.m.

Laguna Playhouse
606 Laguna Canyon Road, Laguna Beach, 949-497-2787; www.lagunaplayhouse.com
The oldest running playhouse on the West Coast, this 1920s-era theater presents every kind of theatrical event imaginable, from dramas and comedies to musicals and children's theater. Make time for a performance before or after dinner and don't forget your swimsuit; the theater is just steps from the beach.

Redfern Gallery at Montage Resort
30801 S. Coast Highway, Laguna Beach, 949-715-6193; www.redferngallery.com
In addition to impeccable accommodations and spectacular views, the Montage Resort also houses the Redfern Gallery, which features early California impressionist painting. Here, you'll find the likes of Granville Redmond's "Patch of Poppies," a lovely painting of a hill with California poppies and lupines looking up to a clouded sky that is reminiscent of Claude Monet's "The Poppy Field, near Argenteuil."

drive
As you leave Laguna Beach, head back to the coastal drive along the South Coast Highway (Route 1) toward I-5 for the most direct way to return to San Diego. If you're looking for more than a coastal drive, however, there is another route you can take that will surely surprise, if not delight you. You must sidetrack by taking an inland route via the Laguna Canyon Road to Highway 73 South. As you drive away from the ocean, you'll begin to think you're heading straight into the mountains.

As you advance toward Highway 73 South (which will take you to back to the I-5), the tall hills transition into California's distinctive chaparrals as well as what resembles rolling pastures of the Midwest more than a California coastline. This is a particularly good option in springtime when many of the surrounding hills are carpeted with pastel and gold wildflowers. Winter rains replenish southern California's dry hills with vegetation and by spring, you will likely see spots of golden, almost neon orange along the landscape. These are bunches of the golden poppy, California's state flower. You might also catch a peek at sprays of pale purple that are the lupines that grow throughout the area.

Laguna Beach lifeguard tower ▪ Sapphire dining room ▪ Sapphire restaurant ▪ The Ritz-Carlton Spa

If you choose the coastal option on Highway 1, you'll pass Dana Point and San Juan Capistrano before reconnecting with I-5, which will take you through San Clemente, where **Trestles Beach**, a prized surfing spot, is located. The village of San Clemente may be a good place to stretch your legs, since you'll face at least a 30-minute drive through San Onofre and the Camp Pendleton Marine Corps Base before you hit Oceanside in San Diego County. As the last bastion of Orange County's charming coastal towns, San Clemente prides itself as the "Spanish Village by the Sea." Indeed, the city's proximity to the early Spanish mission San Juan Capistrano mirrors its Spanish influence. The coastal community is complete with such Spanish-style structures topped with red villa tile roofs. Head to Avenue Del Mar to watch artists paint at San Clemente's monthly Art Walk, which takes place on the last Thursday of every month at 5:30 p.m. The walk will take you to San Clemente's pier as well.

As you continue south, the landscape will become less lush with the approach of San Onofre State Beach. Popular as a campground and surfing beach, San Onofre is a good place to make a stop or take a final photo before entering San Diego County. As you drive along San Onofre State Beach, you'll notice how it's considerably secluded from the modest hubbub of its northern neighbors in Orange County. Exit at Basilone Road off the I-5 to get to the beaches and where you will surely run into some veteran surfers who flock to Trestles for its memorable waves—and ever memorable coastline, where San Diego begins and Orange County ends.

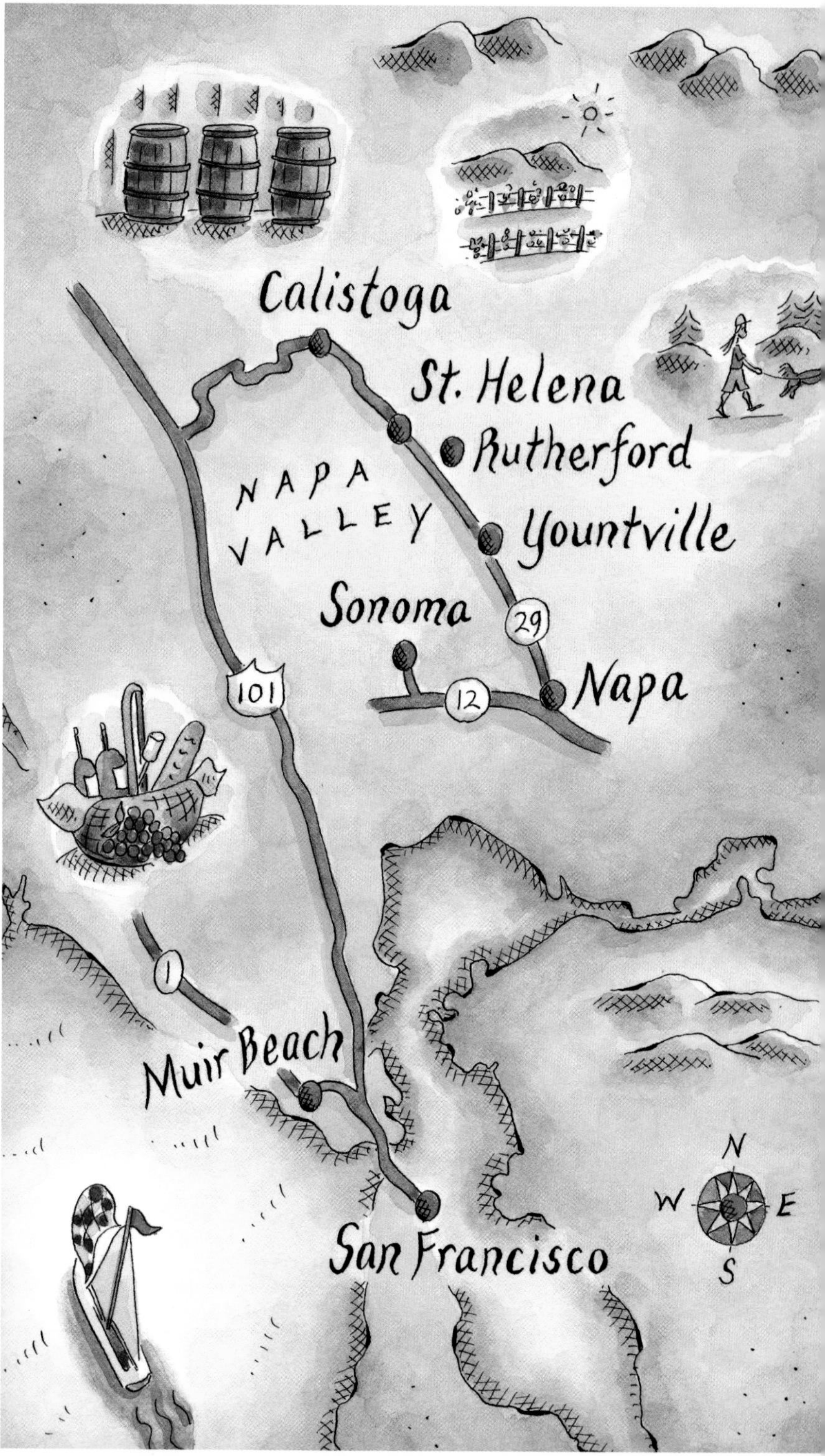
Calistoga
St. Helena
Rutherford
NAPA VALLEY
Yountville
Sonoma
29
Napa
101
12
1
Muir Beach
San Francisco
N
W
E
S

CHAPTER 8
SAN FRANCISCO TO NAPA

The Napa Valley is filled with some of life's greatest pleasures—the wine is plentiful, the food is some of the best you'll find in the country, and there's something about the scenery that makes the valley seem much farther away from the city than it really is (only 45 miles). All of these things combine to make Napa an irresistible weekend away for the 5 million people who descend on the valley each year. It doesn't matter if you're a serious connoisseur or don't know the difference between a burgandy and a brut; both types of people populate the wineries' tasting rooms to sniff, swirl and sip, before retiring to one of the local restaurants at night for even more wine and mouthwatering cuisine. Several outstanding chefs have set up camp here, including the famed Thomas Keller, who has turned the tiny town of Yountville into something of a culinary mecca. Of course, all of this delicious superabundance means the place can get packed, especially when the weather is warmest (late summer and early fall). August through October is crush (or harvesting time) at the vineyards so the valley is flush with visitors and activity. Consider visiting in the winter or early spring. You'll likely need a warm sweater or coat but you'll encounter less traffic on the roads and in the wineries and restaurants.

starting out

Take in San Francisco for a night or two from a Mobil Five-Star hotel: **The St. Regis San Francisco** (*125 Third St., San Francisco, 415-284-4000; www.stregis.com*) is one of the city's newest luxury hotels with stylish rooms that most decorators would clamor to claim as their own. **The Four Seasons Hotel San Francisco** (*757 Market St., San Francisco, 415-633-3000, 800-819-5053; www.fourseasons.com*) also features a contempory design and is located near Union Square's shopping. Or get an elegant night's sleep in Nob Hill at the **The Ritz-Carlton, San Francisco** (*600 Stockton St., San Francisco, 415-296-7465, 800-241-3333; www. ritzcarlton.com*).

drive

Start your drive early—you'll miss much of the traffic flowing in and out of San Francisco. While there is still a chill in the air, head out of the city by going north on Highway 101. The low-hanging fog around the Golden Gate Bridge is the perfect image to erase the traffic-clogged city behind you.

Pool at The St. Regis • San Francisco skyline • Victorian Houses • The St. Regis

If you prefer to drive directly to the Napa Valley, continue on 101 about 24 miles until the turnoff for Napa. But if you have several hours and the desire to explore some of the beautiful Pacific coastline, take the CA-1 exit toward Stinson Beach/Mill Valley about 8.5 miles after crossing the Golden Gate. Once you've left the cityscape, CA-1, with its fragrant eucalyptus trees, will quickly take you into the hillsides of Tamalpais Valley. As you head north along the coast, there are a couple of good stops along the way.

see

Muir Beach

www.muirbeach.com

When the road finally flattens and straightens out (about 20 minutes from San Francisco), follow the turnoff on your left for Muir Beach. This pictur-esque strip of sand is part of the Golden Gate National Recreational Area. The spectacular view from the top of the bluffs alone is worth this small de-tour in your trip. Unlike Stinson, a much larger surfer beach that you'll pass later on CA-1, Muir Beach can be positively tranquil, especially if you visit on a weekday. When the weather turns warmest in August and early fall, the parking lot fills up quickly—as does the beach with picnicking families.

eat
★★★The Pelican Inn
10 Pacific Way, Muir Beach, 415-383-6000; www. pelicaninn.com

Adjacent to the turnoff to Muir Beach, you'll notice the quaint Tudor-style Pelican Inn. It's a great place for an early—and hearty—lunch. Since you'll most likely get your fill of French bistro cuisine and wine in Napa, indulge here in English brews and comfort food: prime rib and Yorkshire pudding, Beef Wellington, bangers and mash, and shepherd's pie, among other classic dishes.
Pub menu. Lunch, dinner. $

drive

After lunch, it's back on CA-1 to snake further north along the coast. For a longer detour, continue on the road until you get to Point Reyes Station, a small town about 30 miles north of San Francisco that is the gateway to the **Point Reyes National Seashore**. Point Reyes Seashore tends to be one of the more wind-swept beaches in northern California but it offers a fantastic view of the Pacific and the surprisingly underdeveloped coastline.

From Point Reyes, follow CA-1 north alongside the coastal estuary of Tomales Bay. This road will eventually lead to a turnoff for Bodega Highway and then CA-12, which you'll take east through the charming town of Sebastopol. Technically, once you enter Sebastopol, you're in wine country. But instead of stopping here, enjoy the drive through town and Santa Rosa because the main attractions are about an hour and 45 minutes north. In Santa Rosa, you'll get back on Highway 101 North for about five miles and then take the exit toward River Road. At Mark W. Springs Road, turn right and continue on Petrified Forest Road until you reach Foothill Boulevard.

stop

The Napa valley is 30 miles long and includes the towns (from north to south)of Calistoga, St. Helena, Rutherford, Oakville, Yountville and Napa. There are two main roads that run north-south through the valley. The first option—CA-29 on the west side—may look like the more efficient of the two, but it's well-traveled so this route is significantly slower when traffic is heavy. The Silverado Trail, which meanders along the east side of the valley, is a bit more winding, attracts fewer drivers and offers spectacular views of the countryside. It's worth noting, however,

SAN FRANCISCO
CABLE CAR

that the locals on this road tend to take the curves at speeds well above the speed limit and won't hesitate to pass cars that don't do the same. Numerous cross-valley roads will take you between these two main roads.

CALISTOGA

They're easy to overlook these days, but more than 100 years ago, the area's hot springs were the attraction that drew visitors to Napa Valley—not the wine. In the tiny town of Calistoga, the volcanic muds and geothermal waters are still main attractions. Most tourists head straight for Old Faithful, the other so-named gushing geyser that erupts as if on cue about every 40 minutes. Skip this tourist trap and instead appreciate the region's geological delights later with a sumptuous visit to a spa. Downtown Calistoga, with its quaint shops and restaurants, is a perfect place to get out of the car and stretch your legs. Lincoln Avenue is the main strip and you'll find numerous art galleries and artisan wares.

Pool at Calistoga Ranch • Napa Valley • Dining room at Calistoga Ranch • Calistoga

stay

★★★★Calistoga Ranch

580 Lommel Road, Calistoga, 707-254-2800,
800-942-4220; www.calistogaranch.com

This 46-room resort offers a quiet retreat after a day spent exploring local vineyards. Each room is housed in a free-standing lodge, decorated using natural materials with fireplaces, plush beds topped with down duvets and private outdoor showers. The onsite restaurant has an American menu created by chef Eric Webster which is paired with local wines. A chef is also available to prepare a private dinner in guest lodges. The Bathhouse spa offers a full menu of luxurious treatments while the fitness center, yoga deck and organized hikes keep guests entertained.
46 rooms. Restaurant. Fitness center. Spa. $$$$

eat

★★Wappo Bar and Grill

1226 Washington St., Calistoga, 707-942-4712

A charming bistro located in a small yellow house with a beautiful tree-lined courtyard, this restaurant offers small and large plates that run the culinary gamut. Nibble on everything from Thai coconut curry with prawns and vegetables to tandoori chicken with lemon basmati rice. In warmer weather, snag a seat on the charming outdoor patio.
International menu. Lunch, dinner. Closed Tuesday. $$

spa

★★★★The Bathhouse

580 Lommel Road, Calistoga, 707-254-2820;
www.catogaranch.com

The northern California town of Calistoga is famous
for its natural hot springs and mineral clay baths.
The Bathhouse at Calistoga Ranch was opened in
2004 by the group behind sister property Auberge
du Soleil and features five treatment rooms, inspired
by the native landscape and designed with organic
elements such as copper, stone, wood and water.
Four of the treatment rooms feature large terraces
with soaking tubs and showers, and all are tailor-
made for treatments involving a bath: buttermilk
baths, mud baths or thermal mineral pool soaks. The
spa draws water from the local hot springs and uses
Napa Valley ingredients, including honey, grapeseed
and bay laurel, in many of the treatments. The mud
wrap promises to boost immunity. Morning yoga
takes place in the resort's wine cave.

THE BATHHOUSE

see

Ca'Toga Galleria D'Arte

1206 Cedar St. (just off of Lincoln Ave.), 707-942-3900;
www.catoga.com

See the works of Italian muralist Carlo Marchiori,
which include ceramics, tiles, paintings, sculpture
and furniture in Classical and Baroque styles. Open
Thursday-Monday.

Hurd Beeswax Candles

1255 Lincoln Ave., 707-942-7410;
www.hurdbeeswaxcandles.com

This charming shop offers demonstrations of candle
making from pure beeswax. Watch the artisans
create their wares and then pick up some brightly
colored, all-natural sticks to take home. Open Sun-
day-Thursday 10 a.m.-5:30 p.m., Friday-Saturday 10
a.m.-8 p.m.

Main Element

1333A Lincoln Ave., 707-942-6347

A welcoming space in downtown Calistoga, this
gallery exhibits upscale, locally made wine country
art and furnishings. Wares include everything from
colorful, hand-blown glass vases to handcrafted
wood rocking chairs. Open daily 10 a.m.-6 p.m.

CA'TOGA GALLERIA D'ARTE

WOODHOUSE CHOCOLATES

ST. HELENA

St. Helena, about eight miles south of Calistoga, is one of several quaint towns along CA-29 and boasts a tiny population of just more than 6,000 residents. The town is the location of the west coast branch of the esteemed **Culinary Institute of America** (*2555 Main St., St. Helena, 800-333-9242*), where you can watch cooking demonstrations and dine on the terrace at the school's Greystone restaurant. As you're driving through St. Helena, CA-29 turns into Main Street, St. Helena's main historic downtown thoroughfare. Here you'll find plenty of shops for browsing—and picking up snacks.

see

The Model Bakery
1375 Main St., St. Helena, 707-963-8192;
www.themodelbakery.com
This bakery is a St. Helena institution, with an 80-year plus history. Don't miss the signature pain levain, cheese baguettes and walnut bread. The shop is also a good place to pick up a picnic lunch, soups and brick-oven baked pizza. Open Tuesday-Friday 6:30 a.m.-6 p.m., Saturday 7 a.m.-7 p.m., Sunday 7 a.m.-4 p.m.

Woodhouse Chocolate
1367 Main St., St. Helena, 800-966-3468, 707-963-8413;
www.woodhousechocolate.com
This cozy, butter-yellow colored shop sells handcrafted chocolates, truffles and toffees. The business is a family affair, started by a couple and their daughters who left the wine business for the upscale chocolate trade, an effort that has been a sweet success. Daily 10:30 a.m.-5:30 p.m.

Napa Soap Company
651 Main St., St. Helena, 707-963-5010;
www.napasoapcompany.com
Find all-natural soaps made from local Napa Valley ingredients like grapeseed oil, lavender, herbs, beeswax, honey and even a little cabernet. The shop is located just south of downtown. Open daily 10 a.m.-5 p.m.

stay

★★★★Meadowood Napa Valley
900 Meadowood Lane, St. Helena, 707-963-3646,
800-458-8080;www.meadowood.com
On 250 wine-country acres, Meadowood is large, but its staff is attentive—from the esteemed resident

MEADOWOOD

AUBERGE DU SOLEIL

wine tutor to the guest services manager assigned to each arriving visitor. The owners also run Screaming Eagle Vineyards, with a product so exclusive you have to join a mailing list to get a bottle. Enjoy a game of croquet, tennis or golf, or simply lounge by the pool. The suites, cottages and lodges blend classic country style and California sensibilities with their stone fireplaces, skylights, vaulted ceilings, private decks and luxurious bathrooms—not to mention plenty of modern amenities such as flat-screen TVs, DVD/CD players, coffee and tea pots and toasters. The Grill is available for casual dining under the shade of an umbrella, and the Restaurant turns out eager-to-please gastronomic delights.

85 rooms. Wireless Internet access. Two restaurants, three bars. Children's activity center. Fitness center. Spa. Pool. $$$$

RUTHERFORD

Four miles south of St. Helena on CA-29 is the small hamlet of Rutherford, home to one of the top hotels in Napa Valley. While there are plenty of wineries to visit here, one of the best reasons to visit Rutherford is another kind of tasting—olive oil. **Round Pond Olive Mill** (*888-302-2575; www. roundpond.com*) produces some of the valley's finest gourmet olive oils. From CA-29 (southbound) turn left on Highway 128 East/Lake Berryessa/Rutherford Road and follow Rutherford Road for 1.5 miles. Round Pond will be on your left-hand side.

You could easily spend an entire afternoon here. For the full experience, make reservations for the alfresco lunch. For $50 a person (four-person minimum), you'll tour the olive mill and learn about the meticulous cold-press process behind Round Pond's four signature oils: Italian varietal, Spanish varietal, blood orange and Meyer lemon. A guide will lead you through tastings of each paired with vinegars (also made here), fresh organic produce and baguettes. The afternoon is topped off with a family-style lunch of local cheeses, meats, fruits and olive oil cake for dessert. On the third Saturday of every month from noon-4 p.m., purchase fresh olive oil straight from the spigot. Oh yeah, they also make wine at the charming vineyard across the street. Open daily.

eat

★★★★Auberge du Soleil

180 Rutherford Hill Road, Rutherford, 707-963-1211, 800-348-5406;
www.aubergedusoleil.com

This sun-drenched sanctuary is perched on a quiet 33-acre hillside olive grove in Rutherford. What once began as simply a Provence-inspired restaurant in 1981 is now a full-fledged sanctuary. Luxurious touches include Italian linens, flat-screen TVs, wet bars with stocked Sub Zero refrigerators (full-size in suites), espresso machines, large soaking tubs, CD players with a choice of CDs, wine, daily fresh fruit and a personal welcome note. Don't miss the exclusive spa featuring Meyer lemon olive oil massages, among other treats, and the indulgent private Melisse Suite. The accommodations portion of the resort was recently gated to ensure maximum privacy.
52 rooms. Children over 16 only. Wireless Internet access. Restaurant, bar. Fitness center. Spa. Pool. Tennis. Business center. $$$$

Auberge du Soleil ▪ The Auberge Spa ▪ The French Laundry ▪ Dining room at The French Laundry

spa

★★★★The Auberge Spa

180 Rutherford Hill Road, Rutherford, 707-963-1211; www.aubergedusoleil.com

The glorious Napa Valley surroundings have inspired this spa's philosophy, with vineyard, garden and valley themes dominating the treatment menu. Nutrient-rich grapeseed and locally grown herbs and flowers are the foundation for the vineyard's massages, body treatments and facials. Seasonal treatments are also a highlight of a visit to this spa, where a rosemary renewal massage is featured in spring, a luscious peaches and cream body mask in summer, a harvest-inspired cleanse in fall, and a peppermint and eucalyptus body treatment in winter.

YOUNTVILLE

On your way to Yountville further south on CA-29, you'll pass through the tiny town of Oakville and its namesake gourmet **Oakville Grocery** *(7856 Mt. Helena Highway; www.oakvillegrocery.com)*. Though frequented by tour buses and carloads of winery-goers, it's still worth a stop if for nothing more than an afternoon latte. It is considered the place to pack a wine country-worthy picnic with a wide selection of cheese, charcuterie, condiments, sweets and other delicious finds. Meanwhile, Yountville is a

A DAY OF PRIVATE WINE TASTING

There are basically two ways to taste your way through northern California's best wineries: Go elbow-to-elbow with the masses at the open (and for that reason more popular) tasting rooms, or make some reservations ahead of time and enjoy a more intimate experience. Pick a few big name wineries and take the first tactic if spontaneity and meeting new friends are priorities; but if private indulgence is key, consider the following itinerary.

Start in the Stags Leap district, which is known for its cabernet sauvignon, in lower Napa. Make **Hartwell Vineyards** your first stop. You'll see its formidable iron gate and Cyprus tree-lined driveway from the west side of the Silverado Trail. Private tours and tastings ($45 per person) are available Wednesday-Saturday at 11 a.m. and 2 p.m. only. Enjoy cheese, chocolates and pours of Hartwell's library wines, available only at the winery.
5795 Silverado Trail, 707-255-4269; www.hartwellvineyards.com.

About one mile north on the same road, look for a turnoff on the east side that is marked only by several numeric addresses—6126 should be among them. Follow the road back into the hills and eventually you'll come upon one of the more unusual architectural masterpieces in the valley. The famed Viennese artist Friedensreich Hundertwasser designed the whimsical **Quixote Winery** with the idea that Napa needed a winery that didn't take itself too seriously. Your private tour ($25 per person) will explain how this brightly colored tile and stucco building—complete with a giant golden turret—

came to be and include tastings of Quixote's signature petite syrah.
6126 Silverado Trail, 707-944-2659; www.quixotewinery.com

At this point, you're probably getting a little hungry. Make **Robert Sinskey Vineyards** your next stop. Known for its organically farmed vines, this winery takes food pairing seriously. Make a reservation ahead of time for the Bento Box tasting at noon and enjoy a light four-course lunch paired with seasonal wines. $60 per person.
6320 Silverado Trail, 707-944-9090; www.robertsinskey.com.

For an up close view of another Napa Valley architectural gem, continue on the Silverado Trail to the **Castello di Amorosa**. Take Larkmead Lane (there's only one way to turn) across the valley, turn right on CA-29 and take your first left about 400 yards past Peterson Road. This 13th century-style Tuscan castle took 14 years to build using eight tons of hand-chiseled stones sourced locally and in Europe. The details are impressive, like the thousands of handmade bolts for every door, a working well in the courtyard, Italian murals and a massive 500-year-old fireplace. And then there's the wine. The best way to enjoy the Castello is the extensive VIP tour, which will take you away from the crowds, through the 107 rooms and deep into the caves beneath the castle to explain the winemaking process as well as the castle's construction. Finish with a private tasting served with a variety of antipasto dishes and fine wines. $500 for two people.
4045 North St. Helena Highway, 707-942-8200; www.castellodiamorosa.com

BOUCHON

perfect spot for some gourmet sustenance. In fact, it's often referred to as the "culinary capital of the Napa Valley" and with good reason. There's a slew of fine restaurants here. When you're not eating, take a stroll down Washington Street (the main strip) where you'll find inviting inns and quaint shops.

eat

★★★★★ The French Laundry

6640 Washington St., Yountville, 707-944-2380; www.frenchlaundry.com
At this former French steam laundry, chef Thomas Keller has raised the standard for fine dining in America. While the country locale—a circa-1900 rock and timber cottage—makes diners feel at home, tables topped with Limoges china, crystal stemware and floor-length linens, set the tone for the nine-course French or vegetarian tasting menus that change daily but always rely on seasonal produce and organic meats. Dishes are small and prompt contemplation on the perfect marriage of fresh, pristine ingredients on each plate. The affable staff keeps the experience casual and comfortable, yet refined and memorable. Reservations are taken two months in advance, so be prepared if you're hoping to snag a table at this perennially outstanding American classic.
American menu. Lunch (Friday-Sunday), dinner. Closed two weeks in January and one week in late July-early August. Reservations recommended. Jackets required. $$$$

★★★ Bouchon

6534 Washington St., Yountville, 707-944-8037; www.bouchonbistro.com
If you can't get into The French Laundry, try Thomas Keller's more casual French bistro. Like most Napa Valley restaurants, the fare is seasonal, but Bouchon maintains a decidedly bistro flavor, right down to the pommes frites, chalkboard specials and newspaper rack by the nickel bar. You can't go wrong with any of the fresh seafood, and the comfort dishes like slow-braised beef short ribs and croque madame are especially enjoyable. Desserts include pot de crème and profiteroles with vanilla ice cream. Be sure to stop by the next-door Bouchon bakery. The éclairs and macaroons are spectacular.

French menu. Lunch, dinner, late-night. Bar. Business casual attire. Reservations recommended. Outdoor seating. $$$

NAPA

After so much quaintness, the city of Napa can seem overly urban at first glance. Interestingly, the town was named for the valley, not the other way around. But even Napa has its charms. Take the Yountville crossroad over to Silverado Trail to escape the traffic and get a better glimpse of the rolling hills and expansive vineyards. The best place to start is probably COPIA—Napa Valley's equivalent of a cultural museum.

see
COPIA

500 First St., Napa, 707-259-1600, 888-512-6742; www.copia.org
Billing itself as "America's Center for Wine, Food, and the Arts" and appropriately named after the Roman goddess of abundance, COPIA has much to offer. You're free to mill about the two sleekly designed floors. On the ground floor, you'll be offered a free tasting of wine almost immediately upon entry. To the right, the Cornucopia gift shop has a huge selection of cookbooks, Riedel wine glasses, COPIA cookware, and wine and table accessories. Each day the center boasts a full schedule of lectures, cooking demonstrations and exhibits. The in-house theater is a great place to spend an evening enjoying dinner and a movie. Dinner can be had in *Julia's*

Views of the Napa Valley Opera House (far left, left), COPIA, Carneros Bistro and Wine Bar

Kitchen, a restaurant inspired by none other than Julia Child. (You can see an installation of her cookware just outside.) Julia's serves French-American cuisine featuring the fresh produce from COPIA's edible gardens. Daily 10 a.m.-5 p.m.; closed Tuesday.

Downtown Napa

Ride a free downtown trolley that passes through several Victorian neighborhoods—the city has more pre-1906 Victorians than anywhere else in Northern California, which was hit by the big San Francisco earthquake of the same year. The trolley makes stops at COPIA and Napa Premium Outlets. Napa County Landmarks periodically conducts 90-minute guided tours on Saturdays, May through October. Call either the landmarks organization at 707-255-1836 or the Napa Conference and Visitors Bureau at 707-226-7459 for more information.

ANNUAL NAPA VALLEY EVENTS

February – March
Napa Valley Mustard Festival
This celebration was first conceived to enliven the valley during the typically slow winter months. But there's nothing particularly wintry about the area in February and March—in fact, the festival is so named because much of the valley is covered in brilliantly yellow wild mustard flowers. The now popular celebration includes grand dinners, jazz concerts, art exhibitions, a photography contest and wine tasting. For the current year's schedule of events, go to www.mustardfestival.org

July
Summer Music Festival at Robert Mondavi Winery
Past concerts have included Ella Fitzgerald, Tony Bennett, Buena Vista Social Club, New Orleans' Preservation Hall Jazz Band and Aimee Mann. Concerts are held July through August and ticket sales begin in April (*www.robertmondaviwinery.com*).

Wine Country Film Festival
Held over four weekends in July and August, this roving outdoor film festival takes place throughout Napa and Sonoma. Flicks such as *A Fish Called Wanda* and *Honeymoon in Vegas* debuted here, and past celebrity guests such as Gregory Peck, George Lucas and Richard Dreyfuss have dropped by. Tickets range from $6-$20, or $90-$145 for weekend passes (*www.wine countryfilmfest.com*). Wine and gourmet foods are available for purchase.

August
The annual **Music in the Vineyards** three-week chamber music festival features many notable artists-in-residence. Concerts are held at various wineries with tastings at intermission. Tickets on sale in April (*www.napavalleymusic.com*).

December
Traditional Christmas carols are played on rare string, wind and percussion instruments in candlelit intimate wine caves throughout the Napa Valley during the annual **Carols in the Caves** festival. Tickets cost $40 (*www.carolsinthecaves.com*).

The **Yountville Festival of Lights** is a free month-long holiday celebration when quaint Yountville is draped in thousands of tiny lights and residents and visitors linger on the streets to sample culinary treats and wine. Horse-drawn carriages provide transportation on Saturdays.

VINEYARDS IN SONOMA

Napa Valley Opera House

1030 Main St., Napa, 707-226-7372; www.napavalleyoperahouse.org.
The Opera House was opened in 1879 as one of the first "respectable"
venues west of the Mississippi River. The building went dark in 1914 and
was finally renovated and reopened to the public in 2002 after being restored to its former splendor. The show schedule includes everything from
jazz and classical concerts to theater and dance productions.

SONOMA

A visit to wine country wouldn't be complete without making a stop in
Sonoma, which is a short drive west from Napa. If you have more time to
spend in the area, Sonoma Valley offers a whole other slew of wineries to
visit. But if nothing else, plan to drive through Sonoma on your way back to
San Francisco. From First Street in Napa, take CA-29 south and turn right
on Sonoma Highway (follow the signs for CA-12/CA-121S) for five miles.
Take a slight right on Napa Road and then a right at Broadway. This road
will take you directly to Sonoma's historic plaza.

The town was arranged around the 8-acre plaza like a traditional Mexican village because up until 1846, Sonoma was under Mexican rule. Then
on June 14, 1846, a group of settlers rebelled in the "Bear Flag Revolt" and
for a brief 25 days, Sonoma was declared the capital of California. The U.S.
government then annexed California, ending Sonoma's days as the seat
of state government. Today the history of the town is well preserved. City
Hall, built in the heart of the plaza in the early 20th century, is still used and
the **Franciscan Mission San Francisco Solano** (*114 E. Spain St., 707-938-
1519; tours given on the hour between 11 a.m.-2 p.m. on weekends*), dating
back to 1823, is open to the public. In addition to the history, Sonoma's
shops and restaurants are well worth the visit.

see

The Vasquez House Library and Tea Room
414 First St. E., Sonoma,
707-938-0510
Find vintage exhibits and extensive photographic and historical archives on Sonoma's history in this house that dates back to 1850. It was originally built for Civil War hero General Hooker. It's now maintained by the local historical society, which serves homemade pastries and tea to visitors. Open Thursday-Saturday 2-4:30 p.m.

The Wine Exchange of Sonoma
452 First St. E., Sonoma,
800-938-1794, 707-938-1794;
www.wineexsonoma.com
Come here for the vast selection of bottles of wine, or do as the locals do, and head straight to the bar in the back. Also try any one of the more than 250 international beers available. Open daily 10 a.m.-6 p.m., Friday-Saturday 10 a.m.-7 p.m., Sunday 11 a.m.-6 p.m.

Lisa Kristine Gallery
452 First St. E., Sonoma,
707-938-3860;
www.lisakristine.com
A startlingly beautiful collection of photographs taken by San Francisco-based photographer Lisa Kristine on her travels through Asia. Open daily 10 a.m.-6 p.m.

eat

★★★Carneros Bistro & Wine Bar
1325 Broadway, Sonoma,
707-931-2042;
www.thelodgeatsonoma.com
About six blocks south of the Sonoma Plaza, Carneros is adjacent to the Lodge at Sonoma, sharing the circular drive. An extensive wine list, wine bar and wine education classes are offered along with an innovative menu of international fare. An open kitchen runs the length of the dining room. Check for special events and live entertainment and keep an eye out for celebrity bartenders. International/Fusion menu. Breakfast, lunch, dinner, brunch. Bar. Children's menu. Business casual attire. Reservations recommended. Outdoor seating. $$$

Harmony Lounge at the Ledson Hotel
480 First St. E., Sonoma,
707-996-9779;
www.ledsonhotel.com.
Enjoy a light meal of small plates with wine pairings at this grand antique hotel off the plaza. Try the beef carpaccio and duck confit and save room for the pear cabernet tart. Check for live entertainment. American/International menu. Lunch, dinner. Bar. $

drive

When you've had your fill of wine country—at least for this visit—head out of town on Broadway/CA-12. Follow signs for CA-121 South to Highway 37 towards San Francisco. With any luck, traffic on Highway 101 will be minimal and you'll be back over the Golden Gate Bridge after about 40 minutes. Even if you're not so lucky, at least the drive out of Sonoma offers one last glimpse of the sun-splashed, serene countryside. Just keep that in mind once you hit the gridlock.

CHAPTER 9
SAN FRANCISCO TO OAKHURST

Oakhurst is a small—*really* small (population 2,868)—picturesque mountain town bordering the Sierra National Forest and the San Joaquin Valley. Between May and October, most people blow past it on the way to Yosemite, which is just 14 miles to the north. But Oakhurst is not only worth a stop, it's a delightful destination in itself. Oakhurst is home to the spectacular Chateau du Sureau, which includes the trip-worthy restaurant, Erna's Elderberry House, and a fabulous spa. The town is quiet and peaceful with just a gentle hum of activity, and its unique blend of natural beauty and unpretentious cultural sophistication make it a perfect weekend escape from the Bay Area.

The drive to Oakhurst from San Francisco is beautiful year-round (though some high roads may not be accessible during winter), but it's especially so during spring, when the traffic is still sparse (it gets heavier during summer months), and there's a crisp, expectant feel in the air. The foothills are a lush green dotted with yellow and red wildflowers, and in the distance, the Sierra foothills are still capped with snow. Most spring days are warm and sunny, and on clear evenings, the sun casts a purple glow on the mountains and the sky is bright with stars.

starting out

See chapter 8 for places to stay in San Francisco for a night or two.

drive

Oakhurst is about 190 miles southeast of San Francisco (or about a four-hour drive). You'll spend the first hour negotiating Bay Bridge traffic and congestion along 580 through Dublin and Livermore. Once you cross the Altamont Pass (mile 40), stay to the left and merge onto Highway 205. Highway 205 will drop you, at approximately the 80-mile mark, in the town of Manteca.

From Manteca, there are two routes to Oakhurst. One continues east on Highway 120 then south on Highway 49; the other follows Highway 99 south to Merced and then loops back up and travels northeast on Highway 140. The two routes form a circle between Manteca and the town of Mariposa, and it's fun to travel one way there and the other way back. The first option, Highway 120 to Highway 49, is the more scenic and exciting of the two, and a more dramatic start to your weekend.

Sun Sun Wo ▪ Downtown Mariposa ▪ Coulterville ▪ Oakdale Cowboy Museum

Once you enter the agricultural town of Manteca, you'll realize how far away you are from the city. Highway 120, here a narrow two-lane road, cuts through the center of town, making this a good place to stop and stretch your legs, breathe some country air and have a refreshment. Follow Highway 120 through town (1.5 miles), and you'll see open-air markets selling seasonal fresh produce. The first on your right, **Jacob's Fresh Produce** (*10954 Highway 120, Manteca; open everday from 8 a.m. to 6 p.m.*), sells cold drinks and an assortment of flavored nuts, including tequila-flavored pistashios.

As you leave Manteca and continue east along Highway 120, you'll find yourself in horse country. Barns, log cabins and rodeo ads line the road. Approximately 25 miles from Manteca, you'll arrive in the tiny town of Oak-dale, "the Cowboy Capital of the World."

Five miles east of Oakdale, Highway 120 becomes beautiful. The road twists and turns dramatically, climbing up small granite peaks and down into lush valleys. Old stone fences mark off farms and cattle ranches. Eventually the vista opens to views of rolling green hills and, in the distance, the first glimpses of the snow-tipped southern Sierras. As you start to climb, the temperature goes up a few degrees and the air feels drier. Just past Chinese Camp, you'll cross an impressive suspension bridge with breath-

CHATEAU DU SUREAU

taking views of Don Pedro Lake and the Sierra mountains. Keep an eye out for the tiny town of Moccasin. This is where you'll turn off Highway 120 and pick up Highway 49 South.

stop

Just under 10 miles from Moccasin, turn right off of Highway 49 into Coulterville. Isolated and remote, Coulterville feels frozen in time. Original 1800s buildings line Main Street (pretty much Coulterville's only street), including the hotels, saloons and businesses that served an estimated 10,000 residents during the height of the Gold Rush.

If you walk to the end of town (the equivalent of two or three city blocks), you'll see a sign pointing off to the right for "Chinatown." This leads to **Sun Sun Wo** (*5076 Chinatown Main, Coulterville, 209-878-3187*), the town's first general store, owned and operated by Chinese immigrants from 1851 until 1926. It's among the oldest surviving Gold Rush buildings and one of the last adobe structures left in California. For a quick, relaxed lunch, head into the **Coulter Café and General Store** (*5015 Main St., Coulterville, 209-878-3947; Monday-Thursday 7:30 a.m.-3 p.m., Friday-Sunday 7:30 a.m.-8 p.m.*). If it's warm enough, there's a large outdoor patio.

drive

Stretches of Highway 49 from Coulterville to Mariposa are quite steep and treacherous, so this is where you need to stay alert. The lucky passenger, though, will be treated to awesome (and at times nail-biting) mountain views as the road twists and winds through the foothills. Continue south on Highway 49, through miniscule towns like Bear Valley and Mt. Bullion, which you'll miss if you blink. Approximately 30 miles south of Coulterville, Highway 49 takes you through the busy main street of bustling Mariposa. From here, it's a picturesque and relaxing 45-minute drive to Oakhurst.

Oakhurst sits in a valley surrounded by national forests and the Sierra foothills. The town's hub revolves around the intersection of Highway 49 with Highway 41, making a "T." Oakhurst locals are used to the steady stream of traffic, especially during the summer months, when people are headed to Yosemite. After all, Oakhurst's downtown strip, predominantly chain stores, budget hotels and strip malls, doesn't suggest much reason to stay. But if you scratch beneath the surface, you'll see that Oakhurst is more than just a convenient stop on the way to Yosemite. With a burgeoning art community, world-class outdoor sporting activities and a new generation of restaurateurs and winemakers, Oakhurst is coming into its own. Natives are proud to show off the town's rich gold mining history and happy to point you to some unexpected gems.

stay

★★★★★Chateau du Sureau

48688 Victoria Lane, Oakhurst, 559-683-6860; www.chateausureau.com
When you stay somewhere as spectacular as the Chateau du Sureau, it's nice to be in a place that's as quiet and relaxing as Oakhurst, because you'll want to spend as much time as possible simply enjoying the property. Built in 1991, this mansion is a perfect replica of a Provincial French estate. Wrought iron gates swing open to reveal a white stucco castle with a red tiled roof and a stone turret. Perfectly manicured lawns and fountains surround the castle, and practically every window looks out on breathtaking mountain views. On one side of the property, a path leads down to the "park," nine acres of wooded hillside that winds around a small pond and gazebo, overlooks a private boule court, and ends at a life-size chessboard. On the other side of the castle is a small pristine swimming pool. Once you enter the castle, the antique furnishings, iron balconies, fine art, immense fireplaces and oriental rugs, along with impeccable service, will have you feeling like true royalty. On the ground floor, the opulent drawing room has 14-foot ceilings

and a huge blazing fire. The chateau has only 10 guest rooms plus a separate two-bedroom villa. The rooms are exquisitely decorated with antiques from all over the world and luxurious spa-like bathrooms. Each room is named for an herb and has a distinct theme. The "Thyme" room on the ground floor has a king-sized canopy bed and arched windows; the "Lavender" room has a sleigh-bed and private balcony.
12 rooms. Closed two weeks in January. Complimentary full breakfast. Restaurant, bar. Spa. $$$$

eat

★★★★Erna's Elderberry House

48688 Victoria Lane, Oakhurst, 559-683-6800; www.elderberryhouse.com
This world-famous restaurant offers an exquisite seasonal menu of California cuisine. Opened in 1984 by Austrian-born chef Erna Kubin-Clanin, the kitchen serves farm-raised meats and local produce, chosen daily at the farmer's market in Fresno. The prix fixe menu consists of six courses paired with wines from a 725-bottle wine list. Overseen by Erna's daughter Renée, the list includes rare California wines as well as many Austrian selections, in honor of Erna's birthplace. Meals are served in a dramatic, old-world setting of antique French Provincial furnishings, brocade tapestries and original oil paintings.
California, French menu. Dinner. Closed first two weeks in January. Bar. Business casual attire. Reservations recommended. Valet parking. Outdoor seating. $$$$

ERNA'S ELDERBERRY
HOUSE

Yosemite Coffee and Roasting Company

40879 Highway 41, Oakhurst, 559-683-8815;
www.yosemitecoffee.com

For the best coffee in town as well as yummy breakfasts, brunches and sandwiches, pop into the Yosemite Coffee and Roasting Company. The atmosphere and service are no frills (and yes, it's in a strip mall), but the food is fresh and inexpensive; perfect for a quick bite.

American menu. Breakfast, lunch. Casual attire. $

Three Sisters Café

40291 Junction Drive, Oakhurst, 559-642-2253;
www.threesisterscafe.com

In a town of chains and fast food restaurants, this café is a welcome change. Despite the blocky architecture and low stucco ceilings, the place has a warm, welcoming atmosphere and fantastic food. The restaurant is popular with locals, and weekend evenings are comfortably crowded. Chef Richard Beyerl offers a hearty menu of seafood and meat entrées, as well as rich and delicious authentic German specialties such as wiener schnitzel and sauerbraten (German pot roast). The delicious bread is made fresh daily.

Continental menu. Lunch, dinner. Closed Monday-Tuesday. $

spa

★★★★Spa du Sureau

48688 Victoria Lane, Oakhurst, 559-683-6193;
www.chateausureau.com

Decorated throughout in charming Art Deco style, there are only three treatment rooms (all with iPod docks) and one wet room at this petite spa. The standout is the decadent double treatment room with its black marble fireplace, two massage tables separated by translucent drapes, lounge chairs and Jacuzzi. The spa also features a Hydrostorm shower system—one of only a handful in the country—that uses aroma and color therapy aquatics. The treatment menu spotlights traditional European Kur baths, which include marine hydrotherapy and mineral rich baths and use only top-notch ingredients, such as moor mud from the Czech Republic, which is touted for its high concentration of vitamins and minerals.

CHATEAU DU SUREAU
BEDROOM

ERNA'S ELDERBERRY HOUSE

see

Gallery Row

40982 Highway 41, Oakhurst

Oakhurst has a burgeoning and active art community that includes established painters, sculptors, nature photographers and musicians. Six of the town's galleries are conveniently located next to one another in a funky, western-style strip mall off of Highway 41 just north of town. Local favorites include Stephen Stavast (particularly his rock and water series) and David Ashcraft's landscape and abstract photography. Thursday-Monday, 10 a.m.-5 p.m.

Fresno Flats Historical Park

School House Road and Indian Springs Road, Oakhurst,
559-683-6570; www.fresnoflatsmuseum.org

For a glimpse into Gold Rush living conditions and architecture, visit the Fresno Flats Historical Park west of downtown. The museum complex is a collection of homes and buildings dating to the 1870s, most of which were moved to the complex from neighboring towns. You can walk through the various buildings, including a jail, a one-room schoolhouse and a barn, on your own or join a docent-led tour. Monday-Friday dawn-dusk; museum guided tours: Saturday and Sunday noon-4 p.m., Monday-Friday 10 a.m.-3 p.m.

Lewis Creek Trail Head

Highway 41, just north of Cedar Valley Drive, Oakhurst

The Lewis Creek Trail is a woody, peaceful 3.7-mile hike through the Sierra National Forest. Drive north on Highway 41 for approximately four miles and the parking lot for the trailhead will be on your right. The trail quickly crosses the creek, and then you can follow the river south or, if you're feeling energetic, climb the ravine. It's a beautiful path, dense with sugar pines, oaks and cedar trees, and the soothing rushing sound of the creek. For weather and trail information, call the Sierra National Forest Range District at 559-658-7588 or visit www.fs.fed.us/r5/sierra.

Yosemite

209-372-0200; www.yosemite.org

Yosemite is one of the most popular and best-known national parks in the world, and the south entrance is only about 15 miles from Oakhurst. At this south entrace, you'll find one of the park's great attractions, Mariposa Grove. This is the largest and most visited of Yosemite's three groves of giant sequoia trees. The two-mile road to the grove is closed to cars from November to April, depending on conditions, but can be walked, skied or snowshoed anytime. The Grizzly Giant in Mariposa Grove, 209 feet high and 34.7 feet in diameter at its base, is estimated to be 2,700 years old. And that's just the beginning of what you can see in this majestic park; set aside an entire day to hike, bike or tour the park by bus.

Spa du Sureau ▪ Lake McClure ▪ Yosemite National Park ▪ Bay Bridge

Wine tasting at Queen's Inn by the River

41139 Highway 41, Oakhurst, 559-683-4354; www.queensinn.com

Plan to spend an evening tasting wine at Queen's Inn by the River. This charming and lively wine and beer garden is in a small rustic cabin over-looking the Fresno River and offers an impressive variety of European and California wines as well as an extensive beer list. There's an outdoor beer garden with views of the river. The Inn is just north of town off of Highway 41, but like many Oakhurst addresses, it's easy to miss the sign, and the dirt road leading down to the river is so poorly marked you'll wonder if you've made a mistake. But keep going. The road ends in a parking lot right next to the inn. Wednesday-Saturday 4-10 p.m.

drive

Your drive home begins by backtracking along Highway 49 for approximately 30 miles to Mariposa. If you drove straight through Mariposa on the way to Oakhurst, it's worth stopping for lunch or at least a coffee this time through. Mariposa is a historic western town where, in 1839, Kit Carson discovered Mariposa Mines, the first hard-rock mines found during the Gold Rush. Originally populated by Native Americans, Mariposa—Spanish for "butterfly"—was settled practically overnight by throngs of immigrants looking for gold. Today, the small town has fewer residents than it did in the 1900s. Mariposa's charming main street is full of antiques, galleries and gift shops, and has retained most of the original 19th-century buildings.

YOSEMITE'S MERCED RIVER

Turn onto 7th Street for lunch at the **River Rock Inn and Deli Garden Cafe** (*4993 7th St., Mariposa, 209-966-5793, 800-627-8439; summer 7 a.m.-9 p.m.; winter 7 a.m.-5 p.m.*) for a coffee and muffin just across the street at **Pony Expresso** (*4996 7th St., Mariposa, 209-966-5053; Monday-Friday 6:30 a.m.-5 p.m., Saturday 7 a.m.-3 p.m., Sunday 7 a.m.-2 p.m.*). Leaving Mariposa, pick up Highway 140 south, which you'll follow for about 40 miles to Merced. The drive is scenic and peaceful through rolling green hills dotted with yellow wildflowers. You'll pass grazing sheep and cattle, and an Andalusian horse farm. The approach to the city of Merced, also known as "The Gateway to Yosemite," is flat and straight, with green fields on each side of the highway stretching for miles.

At Merced, pick up Highway 99 north, which will take you back to Manteca, where you'll pick up Highway 205 and then Highway 580 to the Bay Bridge. From Merced, it will take you just over two hours to get back to San Francisco. As you leave the mountains behind, the Highway picks up speed and becomes more and more industrial, but it's an easy, straight drive, leaving you free to reminisce about your perfect weekend getaway.

CHAPTER 10
SAN JOSE TO BIG SUR

Big Sur, the narrow 90-mile strip of land that runs from Carmel, California, in the north to San Simeon in the south is one of the most breathtaking shorelines in America. Known for dramatically sheer cliffs, thickly forested wilderness and powerful surf that thunders across the shore and churns over ocean-strewn rock formations, Big Sur has attracted all types, from artists to aristocrats who, bound by their love of nature, have protected the area from overdevelopment. The result is a certain kind of magic that only a road trip can reveal. Each hairpin turn along the coast reveals one glorious view after another—and there's nothing like a stay at a place like the Post Ranch Inn, which teeters off a cliff for even more incomparable views from a cocoon of luxury. We've included a few great stops along the way, including an overnight stop (if you choose) in charming Carmel-by-the-Sea.

starting out

If you're flying in for your Big Sur vacation, San Jose is the closet major airport. And while the city has plenty to offer, the reason you've come is to enjoy the coast. So don't dawdle in San Jose (save that for another trip). Make a beeline for California Route 17 South on your way down to Carmel. There is much to see and do.

stop

Though just out of the vacation gate and barely 10 miles from San Jose, you'll come to your first stop—the quaint town of Los Gatos. On a sunny day, the town center's walkways brim with window shoppers browsing antiques shops, art galleries, chic boutiques and occasionally stopping at **Powell's Sweet Shoppe** (*35 N. Santa Cruz Ave., Los Gatos*) for an old-fashioned treat. You won't see your typical chain retailers and eateries in Los Gatos (there is a Banana Republic, but you'd barely recognize it). Storefronts and restaurants are impeccably kept up in bright taxi-cab

Scenic coastal road in Carmel-by-the-Sea • Thatched cottage • Dolores Street shops • Point Lobos

yellows, terra cottas, pinks and other cheerful colors. Residents like to live well with an eye to health—even pets are treated to soy-based bones at the town pet store. Their owners can sample organic coffee at the local favorite **Los Gatos Coffee Roasting Company** (*101 W. Main St.*), which makes rich, flavorful brews you can take with you on the road.

drive

If Los Gatos already has you in the vacation mindset with its charm, your next stop, Byington Vineyard and Winery, will take you a world away with its views. From Los Gatos, continue south on Route 17 following the signs towards Santa Cruz.

see

Byington Vineyard and Winery

21850 Bear Creek Road, Los Gatos, 408-354-1111; www.byington.com
From Route 17 South, exit Bear Creek Road and head about 5 miles uphill. Use caution as you wind your way up this narrow two-lane road; there are few pull-outs and plenty of shrub-shrouded blind turns as you go and locals who know the mountain can appear in the oncoming lane rather suddenly. Follow the double yellow line toward Boulder Creek. You'll first pass

David Bruce Winery on your right. After a couple more turns, take your left into the Byington parking lot.

If you like a good cabernet, Byington Vineyard and Winery is at the top of its game. Perched at the summit overlooking the vast valley below, Byington—with its ivy-covered stone façade, outdoor patio and bocce ball court—looks like it was transported from the European countryside. Tastings are free and tables are set up on the second-story terrace as well as the lawn—all equipped with wide-open views of the valley below and ridgelines in the distance. Before you depart, take a short spiral pathway to Wedding Hill where lucky brides and grooms can exchange vows surrounded by jasmine and overlooking vineyards, redwood forests and the Monterrey Bay. Open daily 11 a.m.-5 p.m. for tastings

drive
By now, you should already feel like you've been gone for days and you haven't even glimpsed your first up-close coastal view. So get back in the car, retrace your steps back to Route 17 South, and follow it until you hit world-renowned Highway 1 on your way to your stop for the night.

stop
Officially known as Carmel-by-the-Sea to distinguish if from Carmel Valley (which is, not surprisingly, a few miles inland in the valley), Carmel is the northern-most point of the 90-mile coastal stretch known as Big Sur. In addition to its Provincial-style charm, and one of the greatest beaches in

CALIFORNIA STATE ROUTE 1 (HIGHWAY 1)

California Highway 1 is so special, the U.S. government has designated it one of only 27 All-American Roads—byways with features so unique they are worthy of visiting as scenic or historic destinations unto themselves.

The stretch of blacktop that traces the shoreline of Big Sur is a narrow, winding, two-lane road that hugs the mountains heading north and the coastline heading south (often just a few feet from the precipitous drop to the craggy beaches and ocean below). Lengths of Highway 1 have been given different regional names (you'll see signs that you're on Cabrillo Highway from the San Francisco area through south of Carmel). With few inland highway junctures to the East and nothing but ocean and seaside stops to the West, you have to try to get lost. Mile after mile of ocean, mountain, field and forest views remain unobstructed by development—a fact that's almost as awe-inspiring as the stunning vistas themselves.

Central California, Carmel is famous for a few other things: its thriving arts community, efforts to curb development to maintain its character, and its former mayor, Clint Eastwood. Other famous Carmel-enthusiasts have included photographer Edward Weston, novelists Jack London and Upton Sinclair, and actresses Kim Novak and Doris Day, who is still active in the Doris Day Animal Foundation and partial owner of the dog-friendly Cypress Inn.

Though plenty of rich and famous have settled in this town, there's nothing uppity about Carmel's residents. People are approachable and friendly—you can chat with interesting locals at nearby tables during dinner, or keep to your quiet, romantic self.

Carmel is a walking town. In fact, many establishments list only their cross streets, not street addresses, for navigation. The town center runs the length of Ocean Avenue, which takes you from Highway 1 all the way to the dead end at Carmel Beach, which is a good place to develop an appreciation for this seaside town. Carmel offers a host of high class accommodations, and most of them are well within walking distance to the town center.

ALTERNATE ROUTE—SANTA CRUZ

If you want to indulge the kid in you—or actually have kids with you—consider taking an alternate route to Carmel. From Byington, continue south on Route 17 until you find yourself in the bohemian town of Santa Cruz. There are three main attractions here: shopping, eating and strolling the boardwalk (unless you're a surfer; then there are four).

The town's Pacific Avenue is chock full of shops and eateries, but the main attraction in Santa Cruz is the nearby boardwalk, an old-fashioned stretch of planked pathway lined with carnival rides and attractions. To take it all in, park at the Santa Cruz lighthouse and view the boardwalk and its Ferris wheel from this vantage point before walking downhill. Below you, experienced surfers in wetsuits will bob up and down.

A brisk walk downhill takes you to the boardwalk, packed daily with cyclists, joggers and even performers on stilts. Besides the Ferris wheel, there are classic rides such as a wooden roller coaster and bumper cars, and traditional treats like fresh-spun cotton candy.

BERNARDUS LODGE VINEYARD

stay

★★★★Bernardus Lodge
415 Carmel Valley Road, Carmel Valley, 831-658-3400; www.bernardus.com
Long considered one of the finest winemaking estates in California, Bernardus Lodge has a scenic Carmel Valley location and cozy guest rooms, which include feather beds, fireplaces and oversized bathtubs for two. Upon arrival, guests are immediately greeted with a vintage wine and cheese welcome spread. The refined yet casual décor features richly upholstered furnishings, plank flooring and exposed ceiling beams. Each room is appointed with antique armoires and French doors that lead onto a private garden patio or balcony. The spa offers a wide variety of treatments and the meditation garden is an ideal spot to enjoy the picturesque California hillside. The lodge's formal restaurant, Marinus, is an epicurean's delight serving up succulent dishes such as slow cooked duck egg, black trumpet and duck prosciutto, and Dungeness crab cannelloni.
57 rooms. Wireless Internet access. Two restaurants, bar. Fitness center. Spa. Pool. Tennis. Airport transportation available. Business center. $$$$

★★★Mission Ranch
26270 Dolores St., Carmel, 831-624-6436, 800-538-8221;
www.missionranchcarmel.com
Clint Eastwood bought this 1850s farmhouse and saved it from demolition in the 1980s. Since then, it has been restored, expanded and filled with antiques and custom-designed rustic pieces. The cozy guest rooms have quilted beds and some have patios from which to enjoy tranquil sunsets.
31 rooms. Complimentary continental breakfast. Restaurant, bar. Fitness center. $$

SPA AT QUAIL LODGE

MARINUS

★★★Cypress Inn

Lincoln Lane and Seventh St., Carmel, 831-624-3871, 800-443-7443; www.cypress-inn.com

Built in 1929, this landmark Mediterranean-style hotel is only steps from the town center's boutiques, art galleries and great restaurants. A courtyard off the main lobby welcomes dogs and cats, and the inn also offers pet-sitting services. (Hollywood actress and animal advocate Doris Day is a co-owner.) Two floors of guest rooms are not particularly spacious, but they aim to please with pet blankets, fresh flowers, fruit bowls and Sherry decanters.

44 rooms. Complimentary continental breakfast. High-speed Internet access. Restaurant, bar. Fitness center. $$

★★★Highlands Inn, A Hyatt Hotel

120 Highlands Drive, Carmel, 831-620-1234; www.highlandsinn.hyatt.com

Open since 1917, this sophisticated rendering of a mountain lodge is well suited to its rustic setting. Set on a hillside, the hotel looks out on the iconic Carmel surf. The property incorporates an abundance of wood and stone, and the rooms and suites are outfitted in contemporary, earth-tone furnishings.

48 rooms. Wireless Internet access. Two restaurants, bar. Business center. $$$$

★★★Quail Lodge Resort & Golf Club

8205 Valley Greens Drive, Carmel, 831-624-2888, 888-828-8787; www.quaillodge.com

Set on 850 acres on the sunny side of Carmel Valley, the resort's grounds include rolling hills, lakes and gardens. Golfers come for the fantastic 18-hole course designed by Robert Muir Graves and a 7-acre driving range. The Carmel River gently snakes along the course, making it a particularly scenic round. Others take to the three tennis courts and two outdoor pools or retreat indoors to the spa for its wonderful assortment of facials, massages and salon services. The rooms deliver serious comfort: plasma TVs, luxurious bath amenities, complimentary fruit bowls and more. One of two restaurants, the Covey, stands out for its lakeside setting, gourmet cuisine and extensive wine list.

97 rooms. High-speed Internet access. Two restaurants, two bars. Airport transportation available. $$$$

eat

★★★The Covey
8205 Valley Greens Drive, Carmel, 831-620-8860, 888-828-8787; www.quaillodge.com

At this recently renovated upscale eatery within the Quail Lodge Resort and Golf Club, regionally raised poultry and meats join locally caught fish and shellfish on the wine country menu. Indulgences abound, from Sonoma duck with fava bean purée to Monterey Bay red abalone and artichoke cannelloni. Indoor and terrace seating overlook a lake and an arched bridge, where couples often get married.
California menu. Breakfast, dinner. Bar. Business casual attire. Reservations recommended. Valet parking. Outdoor seating. $$$

★★★The French Poodle
Junipero and Fifth Avenues, Carmel, 831-624-8643

This restaurant is a small, intimate hideaway known for artfully presented, mouthwatering fare prepared in the French style. Sample truffles, foie gras, filet mignon and fresh, local abalone.
French menu. Dinner. Closed Sunday. Business casual attire. Reservations recommended. $$$

★★★★Marinus
415 Carmel Valley Road, Carmel Valley, 831-658-3595; www.bernardus.com

This warm, country inn-style restaurant located in the Bernardus Lodge has exposed-beam ceilings, earth-toned walls, vintage tapestries and a magnificent 12-foot-wide European limestone fireplace—plus a patio and surrounding gardens. Dishes use organic and fresh ingredients, and may include turbot with caramelized endive and celery root purée, and local spot prawns with crispy marinated vegetables and truffle vinaigrette. The impressive wine cellar stocks more than 1,000 selections.
California menu. Dinner. Business casual attire. Reservations recommended. Valet parking. $$$$

spa

★★★★The Spa at Bernardus Lodge
415 Carmel Valley Road, Carmel Valley, 831-658-3560, 888-648-9463; www.bernardus.com

This spa has seven treatment rooms, an open-air "warming pool" and a meditation garden with bubbling fountains. Indigenous herbs, flowers, essential oils and healing waters are incorporated into the spa's services. Couples can opt for the vineyard romance treatment, which includes a harvest crush body exfoliation, lavender-grape seed bath, warm grape seed oil massage and a tea service of grape seed herbal tea. In keeping with the winery theme, the chardonnay facial is an 80-minute, hydrating treatment that incorporates chardonnay grape seeds, which are loaded with antioxidants.

see

The Barnyard Shopping Village
3618 The Barnyard, Carmel, 831-624-8886; www.thebarnyard.com

Shop for gifts—or pop into a tasting room or two—at this large shopping center filled with flower gardens and rustic, old-style California barns.

Carmel City Beach
831-624-3543

Located at the foot of Ocean Avenue, this beach has easy accessibility, white sands and surfer-friendly waters. At Carmel River State Beach, south of Carmel on Scenic Road, find calm waters, tide pools and an adjacent bird sanctuary.

BIG SUR

17-Mile Drive

Stretching from Carmel north to Monterey, along the Pacific and through Pebble Beach and the Del Monte Forest, this is one of the most scenic drives in the world.

San Carlos Borroméo de Carmelo Mission

3080 Rio Road, Carmel, 831-624-1271; www.carmelmission.org
The oldest church in Carmel and headquarters for the California missions, this church was founded by Father Junipero Serra, the Spanish Franciscan priest and explorer; it's also his burial place. Monday-Friday 9:30 a.m.-4:30 p.m., Saturday-Sunday 10:30 a.m.-4:30 p.m.

Pacific Repertory Theatre

Mount Verde St. between Eighth and Ninth Streets, plus two additional locations, Carmel, 831-622-0100; www.pacrep.org
The company performs dramas, comedies and musicals in three venues: Golden Bough Playhouse, Circle Theatre, and outdoor Forest Theatre. Schedule varies.

Point Lobos State Reserve

Highway 1, Carmel, 831-624-4909; www.ptlobos.org
This reserve has a natural grove of Monterey cypress plus hundreds of bird and animal species. Picnic area, naturalist programs. No pets. Daily from 9 a.m.; closing times vary.

drive

From Carmel, head south on Route 1. Within a few curves you'll bend around some trees and catch your first view of the ocean at Carmel River, which shows you just how close this road runs to the water. You might audibly gasp because it's so pretty. But that's only the beginning.

stop

Dominated by the Santa Lucia Mountains, the sparsely developed Big Sur region gives nature room to breathe and offers hiking, biking, tide-pool scanning and more. See the rocky Big Sur bluffs, redwood forests, canyons, waterfalls, secluded beaches and sheer mountains—and gain access to several state parks south of Carmel. Just north of McWay Falls on Highway 1 is one of the area's most luxurious and romantic lodgings, the Post Ranch Inn and its famed Sierra Mar restaurant, one of the coast's most gorgeous—and delicious—places to dine and indulge.

Bernardus Lodge spa and grounds (far left and left) • *Post Ranch Inn (right and far right)*

stay

★★★★Post Ranch Inn

Highway 1, Big Sur, 831-667-2200, 800-527-2200; www.postranchinn.com
Perched on a cliff overlooking Big Sur's rugged coastline, the inn is an ideal romantic getaway. Designed to blend with the Santa Lucia Mountains, the buildings resemble sophisticated tree houses. Each of the 40 guest rooms has an ocean or mountain view, king-size bed, wood-burning fireplace, indoor spa tub, private deck and digital music system. The wet and mini-bars are filled with complimentary snacks, juices and half-bottles of red and white wine. What you won't find: TVs or alarm clocks. Wake up when you want to and head to the spa. The Sierra Mar restaurant is superb and has an extensive wine list.
30 rooms. No children allowed. Complimentary breakfast. Restaurant, bar. Fitness center. Pool. Spa. $$$$

★★★Ventana Inn & Spa

Highway 1, Big Sur, 831-667-2331, 800-628-6500; www.ventanainn.com
This stylish resort speaks to nature-lovers with a soft spot for luxury. From its perch 1,200 feet above the coastline on the Santa Lucia Mountains, the property encompasses 243 acres of towering redwoods, wildflower-filled meadows and rolling hills. After swimming, hiking, photo safaris, wild mushroom hunts or a guided Big Sur tour, indulge in a sensational treatment at the spa or dine at Cielo, the resort's restaurant, where the inventive cuisine competes with the impressive view. Afterward, you can hit the Japanese hot baths.

SIERRA MAR

60 rooms. No children allowed. Complimentary continental breakfast. Wireless Internet access. Restaurant, bar. Spa. Pool. Business center. $$$$

eat

★★★ Cielo

Highway 1, Big Sur, 831-667-4242; www.ventanainn.com

This Ventana Inn restaurant shows off nature's bounty, overlooking the coastline from its wide, rustic, outdoor terrace with sturdy redwood tables shaded by market umbrellas. If you can't sit outside, however, the dining room is warm and cozy, with tall windows, a large stone fireplace, wood-beamed ceilings and a bird's-eye view of the exhibition kitchen, where you'll watch as plates of Mediterranean fare are prepared from California's finest ingredients. Starters range from Dungeness crab salad to grilled tiger shrimp with lemon vinaigrette to entrees like peppercorn Ahi tuna, glazed duck breast or applewood-grilled rib eye.

Mediterranean menu. Lunch, dinner. Bar. Casual attire. Reservations recommended. Outdoor seating. $$$

★★ Nepenthe

Highway 1, Big Sur, 831-667-2345;
www.nepenthebigsur.com

This family-run triad of two restaurants (Nepenthe on the top deck, and the more casual Café Kevah below) and a surprisingly eclectic gift shop is a must—whether you want to simply whet your whistle, or sit down to a leisurely meal. The current owners of Nepenthe fell in love with the location, which was once owned by Orson Wells, who bought the property for Rita Hayworth so they could escape Hollywood. Menu favorites include the house-specialty Ambrosia burger, swordfish sandwich and beet salad—all of which go quite nicely with the ocean views to the west.

American, California menu. Lunch, dinner. Bar. Casual attire. Outdoor seating. $$

★★★★Sierra Mar

Highway 1, Big Sur, 831-667-2800;
www.postranchinn.com

At the top of a towering cliff, this acclaimed restaurant is a stunning place to dine, regardless of the weather. The indoor restaurant seating area itself is narrow and seems to follow the coastline upon which the building sits, and that means all the tables have a great view out the floor-to-ceiling windows over the expansive ocean below. Executive chef Craig von Foerster uses seasonal organic products for his Mediterranean/French-inspired menu. And the restaurant boasts one of the most extensive wine cellars in North America. But you don't have to dine here to get a taste of its raw beauty. Sit outside on the small patio for a specialty cocktail, or a glass of wine with the wind breezing over you and the ocean far below. The views from the patio allow you to enjoy the clever "organic architecture" of the various "tree house" cabins that comprise the inn. Visionary architect Mickey Muennig was influenced by Frank Lloyd Wright and it shows in the modern shapes he's blended into the landscape, echoing maritime themes and woodsy outcroppings. California menu. Lunch, dinner. $$$$

CIELO

Deetjen's Big Sur Inn and Restaurant

48865 Highway 1, Big Sur, 831-667-2377;
www.deetjens.com

Since the 1930's, when Norwegians Helmuth and Helen Deetjen built their first barn on this land, the place has sheltered the hungry and tired who found themselves along this rugged undeveloped coast with nowhere else to stay. Slowly, the Deetjens expanded and the inn became a favorite stop for artists, bohemians and travelers of all kinds who shared an appreciation for this wild coast. After Helmuth Deetjen died in 1972, orders were established to maintain the property as it had always been—slanting floorboards, low ceilings, framed news reports, archival photos, and cozy cabin-style redwood rooms included. The inn is on the National Register of Historic Places. But it's not just about the history of this homesteader's haven. Chef Domingo Santamaria conjures up meals from the

INFINITY POOL AT POST
RANCH INN SPA

BIG SUR COASTLINE

goods of local eco-minded farmers and providers that make the wait for a table worth your while. California menu. Breakfast, lunch, dinner. $$$

spa

★★★★Post Ranch Spa
Highway 1, Big Sur, 831-667-2200, 800-527-2200; www.postranchinn.com
This spa focuses on nature-based therapies, from the wildflower facial with organic plants and Big Sur flowers, to the skin-renewing Hungarian herbal body wrap, which blends organic herbs (including sage, ivy, cinnamon and paprika) with a thermal mud body masque. Several treatments also draw from Native American rituals, including the Big Sur jade stone therapy, which uses jade collected from nearby beaches and basalt river rocks to massage sore muscles, and then cooled marble to release inflammation. Private hikes, meditation sessions, yoga and couples massage instruction are also available.

see

Bixby Bridge
The Bixby Bridge, completed in 1932, is one of the highest single-span bridges in the world and straddles a large canyon along the Big Sur coastline. All-weather photographers come to capture this engineering marvel, whether clouds partially obscure the bridge's vast body or sunlight makes its white structural supports gleam.

Julia Pfeiffer Burns State Park
Big Sur Station 1, Big Sur, 831-667-2315; www.parks.ca.gov
Once inside the park, the main attraction, McWay Falls, is a short stroll away. Follow the hordes of people (in Big Sur "hordes" means more than 15) down the chute to the Overlook Trail. Looking back over a sheltered cove, you'll see the 80-foot waterfall flowing off a granite cliff onto the sandy beach below and into the ocean as it crashes to the shore. Follow the path to the end and you'll find a bench. From there, you might be lucky enough to see gray whales on their migratory trails in March, April, December and January. With backcountry trails through redwoods and oaks as well as a 1,680-acre underwater reserve protecting seals, sea lions, otters and other wildlife,

MCWAY FALLS

there's plenty to do in the park. If you're an experienced diver, you can inquire about permits to explore this rich underwater area.

Pfeiffer Beach

Heading south on Route 1, just past the Big Sur Lodge, is Sycamore Canyon Road, barely marked with a yellow turn out sign. Turn right onto this road and drive to the parking lot for Pfeiffer Beach. Even on crisp sunny days, kids run toward the waves lapping up on the beach, while a few hundred yards out, incoming waves explode against the dark jagged rocks littering the cove. Tempting though it might be to take a dip in this wild and cleansing spot, it's best not to due to the strong current. Instead, enjoy the raw power and thunder of the waves, the wind and the amazing mouth of this little cove. While this beach is reputedly a great sunset spot, it can get downright cold—even during the day.

drive

Now comes the hardest part of your trip—deciding where to end. Should you head south to the southern-most point of Big Sur to see Hearst Castle? Head North to go hiking in Andrew Molera State Park, or back to Carmel for more shopping? Or go further north still to the world-famous Monterey Bay Aquarium? If you enjoy the slower pace and flexibility of driving Highway 1, stick with it as you wind your way back north. If you're eager to see what's inland, take Highway 156 east near Castroville. That will take you back to the 101 north where traffic moves faster.

THE NEPTUNE POOL AT HEARST CASTLE

see

Hearst Castle

Highway 1, San Simeon, 800-444-4445; www.hearstcastle.com

If you want to see something awesome beyond the scenery, take the extra time to drive Highway 1 to Simeon for a tour of Hearst Castle. William Randolph Hearst, the media entrepreneur who built a publishing empire on newspapers and magazines, grew up camping on his father's ranch in Big Sur. But by the time he'd amassed his fortune, he decided to add his mark—by building the most opulent castle and grounds in the coastal U.S. Hearst spared no expense, hauling parts of ancient European buildings and the treasures within to adorn his compound. Hearst entertained some of the great figures of his time here, including Winston Churchill, Charlie Chaplin and Cary Grant. The place is completely over-the-top but yet down to earth (witness the ketchup bottles on the dining room table). The indoor pool resembling a night sky is the best part. This landmark is so expansive, and its history so rich, there are five separate tours to guide you through it all. But if you want to marvel in this one-of-a-kind castle, reserve tickets well in advance. Tours depart daily 8:20 a.m.-3:20 p.m.

5 THINGS NOT TO BE MISSED

You can't go wrong on a Big Sur drive. There is something for just about everyone on this idyllic trip. But here are just a few highlights that shouldn't be missed.

1. Byington Vineyard and Winery

Even if you're not in the mood for a taste, stopping off for the view will release your mind from the day-to-day, and prepare you for a fantastic getaway. Pick up a bottle of wine as a memento of the vacation, or as a gift for friends who couldn't make the trip with you.

2. Carmel City Beach

With ever-encroaching developments and shrinking coast-lines, Carmel City Beach reminds you of what a beach should look like. The white sand against the ocean and craggy rocks feels good on your feet and the view does wonders for your soul.

3. Pfeiffer Beach

Though off the beaten path and less promoted than Julia Pfeiffer Burns State Park, this is a different kind of beach from Carmel. This beach allows you to take a walk on the wild side. Take a stroll and feel the mist from waves crashing through keyholes cut in offshore rocks after years of weathering.

4. Nepenthe Restaurant and Phoenix Gift Shop

While many restaurants boast killer views, they can't claim to have been owned by Orson Wells. That and the general vibe at Nepenthe make it worthy of a roadside stop. Even if you're not hungry, a stop at the Phoenix Gift Shop can arm you with trinkets you might not be able to find at home.

5. Sierra Mar at Post Ranch Inn

The modern architecture cleverly built into the landscape. The setting perched at the top of the cliff. The unobstructed views and feeling that you and your fellow guests are in on one of the best kept secrets in the world. Those are the reasons you'll want to stop by for a drink even if you can't get in for dinner or spend the night.

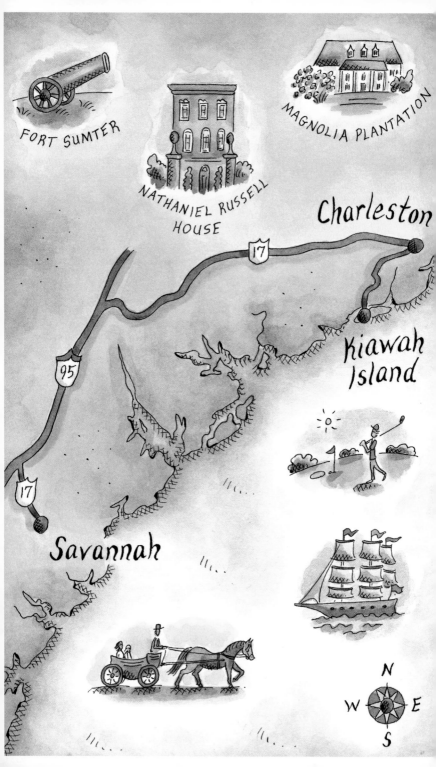

CHAPTER 11
SAVANNAH TO CHARLESTON AND KIAWAH ISLAND

A drive around South Carolina's coastal counties and to the elegant city of Charleston is like returning to a more relaxed and civilized time. This part of the United States is full of history, the people are gracious and lovely, and the sultry weather practically forces you to slow down. As you drive from city to subtropical barrier island, grand old oaks dripping with Spanish moss hang overhead and peaceful marshes line the countryside. Welcome to the low country, where the living is easy year-round. Our route begins in Savannah, takes you to Charleston for a lively evening or two, then from there it's on to Kiawah Island—where you'll see one of the most beautiful beaches with its romantic tidal grasses—and finally back to Savannah, with a stop in picturesque Beaufort. Throw some Pat Conroy paperbacks in your bag and get ready for a low country dance.

KIAWAH ISLAND

starting out

Spend a day in Savannah visiting all the historical sites, parks and "Midnight in the Garden of
Good and Evil" attractions, and then get ready for
a night on the town. Savannah is quite lively after
dark. Tumble into bed at the Mobil Three-Star
President's Quarter's (*225 E. President St., Savannah, 912-233-1600, 800-233-1776; www.president-
squarters.com*), where you'll find inviting rooms
named after presidents, beautiful gardens and
thoughtful touches such as port with turndown
service.

drive

From Savannah, you'll be at the South Carolina
border in just a few miles. Hop on Highway 17N,
the old coastal road, for approximately seven
miles. You can then take Interstate 95 for 30 miles.
This is your typical tree-tunneled interstate, but
it'll shave a little time, and then you'll merge onto
Highway 17N again, where you'll remain for over
60 miles and which is much more scenic and
leisurely. Most of it is a two-lane road shaded by
towering oaks, alternated with patches of hazy
wide-open marshes. You'll also pass several
charming waterfront towns such as Beaufort (see
below) and over bridges, like the one Nick Nolte
is seen driving over in his convertible at the end
of the film *Prince of Tides*. In just over two hours,
you'll start catching a glimpse of Charleston's
low-rise cityscape dotted with spirals and steeples
from the churches. Take the Lockwood Drive exit,
which turns into Broad Street and then hang a left
at Meeting Street to find the recommended hotels
on our list.

stop

Charleston has been called one of the most man-
nerly cities. Indeed, this is what Southern hospitality is all about. The place has all the genteel charm
you'd expect, and then some, but without being
annoying or cloying. Rather, the sweet warm buzz
of Charleston will have you feeling more relaxed
than you've been in a while.

The city manages to strike the perfect mix of
old and new. It has the second largest historical district in North America (behind Savannah).
Preservation is serious business here. Many of
the houses look the same as they did in the early
1800s, but this is a living, breathing city. The doll-

house-pretty homes with large verandas that catch the breeze off the harbor just so are as lived in today as they were back then. Take plenty of time to stroll the residential lanes ("downtown" Charleston is on a peninsula that is less than two miles) to observe all the different types of architecture, including Georgian, Adamesque, Victorian, Italianate and Greek Revival. Most homes have tiny plaques that explain the architecture (residents are used to people stopping and looking). One of the most famous parts of the city is Rainbow Row, named for the burst of pastel colors from the homes that line the streets. These sweet candy-colored homes mostly represent an 18th century Georgian style with arched doorways and gambrel roofs. On East Battery, you'll see magnificent waterfront mansions with "widows" windows where the women used to sit and wait for the ships to come into the harbor. You'll see more of the colonial-style single (just one room wide) and double homes Charleston is known for on Church and Meeting Streets.

For a bit of a rest, duck into one of the churches—you certainly won't have trouble finding one. Charleston is also called the Holy City, thanks to its 187 churches (this divides up into three per block). That's because the city was founded purely as a financial endeavor, not a religious refuge, so there was always a lot of religious freedom. You'll notice that one church, **St. Philip's** (*142 Church St., 843-722-7734; www.stphilipschurchsc. org*), has a large steeple that is leaning slightly to the left—that's from cannonballs that were fired during the Civil War. Another church, **St. John the Baptist** (*120 Broad St., 843-724-8395; www.catholic-doc.org/ cathedral*) is covered in gold stars,

representing the man-hours it took to build it.

One of the most popular activities is a carriage ride, which is a nice introduction to the city. Guides (usually students from the College of South Carolina) take you on a leisurely hoof, casually filling you in on historical facts and points of interest.

stay

★★★★Charleston Place
205 Meeting St., Charleston, 843-722-4900; www.charlestonplace.com
This popular hotel is located in the middle of the historic district, just a stone's throw from Old City Market and King Street, where you'll find the city's best shopping. The enormous 3,000-piece Murano crystal chandelier hanging in the middle of the Georgian open-armed staircase in the lobby is the centerpiece of this buzzing hotel, where people are always zigzagging the Italianate white marble lobby perusing the upscale shops, having drinks in the handsome lounge and heading to the popular Charleston Grille for a bite, before retiring to rooms draped in lace, chintz and damask.
440 rooms. High-speed Internet access. Two restaurants, two bars. Fitness center. Pool. Spa. $$$

★★★Market Pavilion Hotel
225 E. Bay St., Charleston, 843-723-0500, 877-440-2250;
www.marketpavilion.com
This hotel has become the place to stay—or at least have a drink—in Charleston. People crowd the lobby restaurant, Grill 225, for a juicy steak dinner, and then everyone is headed upstairs to the swanky rooftop pool and bar for cocktails and a spectacular view of Charleston and the dark waters. Beautifully appointed guest rooms have four-poster beds,

THE BATTERY

cashmere blankets, marble baths and fluffy bathrobes.
66 rooms. Complimentary continental breakfast. High-speed Internet access. Two restaurants, two bars. Spa. $$$

★★★Planter's Inn
112 N. Market St., Charleston, 843-722-2345; www.plantersinn.com
This polished Relais and Chateaux property, located in the heart of the historic district, has more of a boutique hotel feel, while still offering plenty of old-fashioned charm. The original building, constructed in 1884, was a dry goods supply company; it became a hotel in 1983 and underwent a $4 million renovation in 1997. Rooms have high ceilings, four-poster beds with teddy bears, marble bathrooms and furniture from Baker's historic Charleston collection. Book a junior suite—they're much larger than the regular rooms and have extra large bathrooms. Sweet tea is always available in the comfy lobby, with its velvet couches and oil paintings of historical figures. You'll also find a quiet courtyard with palm trees and a fountain. Rooms facing the courtyard have loggias and rocking chairs.
64 rooms. Restaurant. $$

★★★Wentworth Mansion
149 Wentworth St., Charleston, 843-853-1886; www.wentworthmansion.com
Once a private home, this stately mansion in the city's historic center has hand-carved marble fireplaces, ornate plasterwork and Tiffany stained-glass windows. Cozy guest rooms offer gas fireplaces and charming views. A full European breakfast is served on the porch each morning, and the library is a perfect spot for evening drinks.
21 rooms. Complimentary full breakfast. Restaurant. $$$

eat

★★Anson
12 Anson St., Charleston, 843-577-0551; www.ansonrestaurant.com
This popular low country restaurant in an old warehouse with plantation shutters and gold ballroom chairs is popular with visitors and Charlestoni-ans alike, who come to feast on such favorites as cornmeal-dusted okra

and chicken done three ways: barbequed, fried and braised, and served with collard greens and green tomato marmalade. The chefs use fresh local seafood and produce, often organic, and the menu changes seasonally. You'll also find a nice selection of wines at this Charleston charmer. Southern menu. Dinner. Bar. Children's menu. Business casual attire. Reservations recommended. $$$

★★★★Charleston Grill
224 King St., 843-577-4522; www.charlestongrill.com
Chef Bob Waggoner's French-inspired low country cuisine has earned raves (as well as a cookbook, "Charleston Grill at Charleston Place"). Waggoner divides his menu into four sections: pure, lush, Southern and cosmopolitan, and diners are encouraged to mix and match. For example,

Planter's Inn • Pool at Charleston Place • Wentworth Mansion • Charleston Place guest room

you might pair chilled Maine lobster with micro greens and lemon vinegar (pure) with duck foie gras (lush). The chocolate tasting includes a flight of wine, as does a selection of French cheeses. Live jazz with Quentin Baxter is a big draw Monday through Saturday evenings.
American menu. Dinner. Bar. Children's menu. Business casual attire. Reservations recommended. Valet parking. Outdoor seating. $$$

★★★★Circa 1886
149 Wentworth St., Charleston 843-853-7828; www.circa1886.com
Chef Marc Collins uses regional ingredients to prepare the delightful local cuisine at this restaurant located in the carriage house of the Wentworth Mansion (which was built in 1886). The menu changes but may include Carolina crab cake soufflé, truffle leek fondue and yellow tomato pie. Desserts such as pan-fried Angel food cake and blackberry rice milk panna cotta are always a delightful finish.
American menu. Dinner. Closed Sunday. Bar. Business casual attire. Reservations recommended. Valet parking. $$$

★★Hank's Seafood Restaurant
10 Hayne St., Charleston, 843-723-3474; www.hanksseafoodrestaurant.com
The large platters at Hank's satisfy every craving for seafood—and anything that's deep-fried. The No. 1, for example, includes fried grouper, crumb fried shrimp, fried sweet potatoes and Southern-style coleslaw. As if that weren't enough, there's even fried mashed potatoes. The bouillabaisse and

HIGH COTTON

curried shrimp are less fattening but no less delicious. There's also grilled fish and a raw bar.

Seafood menu. Dinner. Bar. Children's menu. Casual attire. $$

★★★High Cotton

199 E. Bay St., Charleston, 843-724-3815; www.high-cotton.net

"High cotton" is an old Southern saying that means living large, something that the menu here echoes. Boldly flavored dishes such as cornbread-crusted flounder with sweet pea and corn succotash, or bourbon-glazed pork with white cheddar jalapeño grits, are a kick. The live jazz and a popular bar are also big draws, as is the Sunday brunch.

American menu. Lunch Saturday, dinner, Sunday brunch. Bar. Children's menu. Business casual attire. $$

★★★Magnolia's

185 E. Bay St. Charleston, 843-577-7771;
www.magnolias-blossom-cypress.com

This Charleston landmark livens up Southern favorites. The down south egg roll is stuffed with collard greens, chicken and tasso and served with red pepper purée, spicy mustard and peach chutney, while the pan-fried chicken livers come with caramelized onions, country ham and a Madeira sauce. For lunch, try the delicious slow-cooked barbecue mini-sandwiches served on super fresh buns with jalapeño-peach coleslaw.

American menu. Lunch, dinner, Sunday brunch. Bar. $$

★★★McCrady's

2 Unity Alley, Charleston, 843-577-0025; www.mccradysrestaurant.com

You can almost picture the Rutledges having a drink and discussing politics at this handsome restaurant located down a romantic alley in a brick structure built back in 1788. It was originally a tavern before it was abandoned; it was restored to its former glory in 1982, with a few modern touches added, including a sky light and leather banquettes. The menu complements this fresh take. Chef Sean Brock's intoxicating dishes include beef tenderloin with beets, garden onions and smoked hollandaise; halibut with lemon-truffle emulsion; and scallops marinated in mango vinegar, avocado, crispy rice and chamomile. The tome of a wine list includes many hard-to-find varieties. The bar is a sophisticated spot for a glass of wine and a cheese plate, or one of the unusual deserts such as peanut butter cake with popcorn ice cream and salted caramel. Modern American menu. Dinner. Bar. Business casual attire. Reservations recommended. $$$

★★★★Peninsula Grill

112 N. Market St., Charleston, 843-723-0700;
www.peninsulagrill.com

If you're looking for classic Charleston dining, book a table at this classy restaurant with gray velvet walls, golden lighting and windows overlooking the courtyard, in the Planter's Inn. The service is impeccable and the food by longtime chef Robert Carter, including bourbon-glazed jumbo shrimp and cornmeal-crusted trout, doesn't disappoint. The star of the show may be the seven-layer coconut cake—it alone is worth a visit. The champagne bar is another dizzying treat.

American menu. Dinner. Bar. Business casual attire. Reservations recommended. Outdoor seating. $$$

CRAB CAKES AT SLIGHTLY NORTH OF BROAD

★★Slightly North of Broad

192 E. Bay St., Charleston, 843-723-3424;
www.slightlynorthofbroad.net

Better known as SNOB, this rollicking restaurant located in a 19th-century brick warehouse turns out such satisfying dishes as carpaccio of beef with pecorino and grilled bread and crab cakes over a sauté of okra, corn, grape tomatoes and yellow squash.

Low country menu. Lunch, dinner. Bar. Children's menu. Casual attire. $$

Cru Café

18 Pinckney St., Charleston, 843-534-2434;
www.crucafe.com

A guy who buys a place crossing Motley Street and calls it Cru Café has to be one cool cat. This tiny café located in an old Charleston single house is nothing to look at, but don't let that stop you. Make a reservation—even at lunch. The place is packed with people who come to sample owner and chef John Zucker's inventive, fresh cuisine. Try the crunchy calamari salad with slaw and sesame dressing; along with one of the tasty sandwiches and a crisp, cool glass of wine, you have the perfect lunch. If you're sharing, consider the creamy four-cheese macaroni, which arrives at your table

SLIGHTLY NORTH OF BROAD

bubbling hot. Dinner offers pasta and risotto, an à la carte grill, and entrées such as poblano and mozzarella fried chicken. After all this, you might just want a bite of something sweet, like strawberry bread pudding or cheesecake with fresh berries. Rock on.

American menu. Reservations strongly recommended. Casual attire. $$$

Fig
232 Meeting St., Charleston, 843-805-5900; www.eatatfig.com
Fig stands for "Food Is Good" and that pretty much sums up the experience at this deliciously simple restaurant. Chef Mike Lata's philosophy involves combing the best products and technique to extract pure flavor. Witness the local radishes with artisanal butter and braised short ribs with parsnip purée, garden carrots and red wine. The minimalist décor with long banquettes and a communal table sets the mood. Desserts like the olive oil cake with mascarpone and grapes are also just plain, well, good.

American menu. Dinner, late-night. Reservations recommended. Open seating at the bar, counter and community table. $$$

see
Carriage ride
Old South Carriage Company, 14 Anson St., 843-723-9712; www.old-southcarriagetours.com
Besides walking, the best way to see Charleston is by horse-drawn carriage. These one-hour tours will take you along one of four routes in the historic district (which one you

LOW COUNTRY CUISINE

Low country cuisine is more than just fine Southern cooking. The food is a blend of continental dishes fused with bold flavors, using the bounty of ingredients found in the area, including seafood, rice, corn and greens. The cuisine was born when the recipes that the English and French settlers brought over were incorporated with what the slaves from Africa and the West Indies were cooking. You'll find shrimp and grits on practically every menu in town. Once upon a time people ate this for breakfast, lunch and dinner, and it's still the mainstay, as common here as hot dogs are in Chicago or pizza is in New York. Other popular dishes include she-crab soup, catfish stew, Hoppin' John (rice and beans) and Charleston red rice (made with bacon, ham, tomatoes and onions). These days, local chefs continue to use the profusion of available fresh ingredients and the ingenuity that is rooted here to create altogether unique dishes. In fact, Charleston is fast becoming a food destination, hosting wine and food festivals and drawing top chefs from around the country.

get is a toss up; many companies offer the tours but the routes are the same). The unscripted tours are a great way to glimpse the city on your first day. Carriages leave about every 20 minutes. Adults, $20; kids 3 to 11, $13.

CARRIAGE RIDES

Calhoun Mansion
14-16 Meeting St., Charleston, 843-722-8205;
www.calhoumansion.net
It may not be the oldest or the most historic but it certainly is the most over-the-top; and unlike all the other homes you'll tour in Charleston, this one is still lived in. The current owner, a Washington patent attorney, resides here amidst his huge collection of stuff, hosting dinner parties during which music pours onto the street from the veranda, and opening up the doors to tourists who gape at all the loot. You'll find icons, Buddha statues, Tiffany hardware, a collection of taxidermy and everything in between. There is no rhyme or reason to it all; it simply must be seen to be believed, and guides who give the tours with a wink make it even more fun.
Tours run from 11 a.m. to 5 p.m. and cost $15.

The Citadel, The Military College of South Carolina
171 Moultrie St., Charleston, 843-225-3294;
www.citadel.edu
Established in 1842 by an act of the South Carolina General Assembly, the college of nearly 2,000 students enjoys a picturesque setting on the bank of the Ashley River. Stroll the campus and get a sense of the life of a cadet. During the school year, try to come on Friday afternoon at 3:45 to see the military dress parade—widely considered one of the best free shows in Charleston. A small museum portrays the cadet life. Museum: Sunday-Friday 2-5 p.m.; Saturday 12-5 p.m. Free admission. Tours of the campus can be arranged for groups of eight or more; call 843-953-6779 Monday through Friday.

Charleston Museum
360 Meeting St., Charleston, 843-722-2996; www.
charlestonmuseum.org
Founded in 1773 and first opened to the public in 1824, the Charleston Museum claims status as America's first museum. Key artifacts in the collection include an impressive early silver display (George Washington's christening cup is among the pieces), South Carolina ceramics, the chairs that delegates sat in to sign South Carolina's Ordinance of Secession and firearms used in the Civil War.

RAINBOW ROW

NATHANIEL RUSSELL HOUSE GARDEN

Children will enjoy the museums hands-on exhibits. Monday-Saturday 9 a.m.-5 p.m., Sunday 1-5 p.m. Museum: Adults $10, kids 3-12 $5.

Fort Sumter

See where the Civil War began, when Confederacy troops fired onto Fort Sumter on April 12, 1861, after Union forces occupied it. The ferry ride over provides a good history lesson before you arrive. Boats to the fort depart daily at 9:30 a.m., noon and 2:30 p.m. The whole trip is a little over 2 hours; adult tickets cost $15, children 6 to 11 cost $9, and children under 5 are free. Ticket offices open at 8:30 a.m. (Liberty Square) or 9:00 a.m. (Patriots Point). April-Labor Day. Call for hours for the rest of the year. Ferries leave from Patriots Point or the Fort Sumter Visitor Education Center at Liberty Square. Visit www.fortsumtertours.com for more information.

Nathaniel Russell House

51 Meeting St., 843-724-8481; www.historiccharleston.org
This Federal-style brick mansion is like a time capsule. Built by an export/import trade merchant Nathaniel Russell in 1808, the home has only had four owners and is exactly as it was back then—the residence has been restored but never renovated. The "floating" three-story spiral staircase is a wonder.
Monday-Saturday 10 a.m.-5 p.m., Sunday 2-5 p.m. Adults $10

Old City Market

Market Street, between Meeting and East Bay Streets
This alfresco market, said to be open every day since 1782, was a former slaughterhouse (but because this is Charleston, it has an impressive edifice that looks like the Parthenon). Today it's brimming with tourists looking to buy everything from chewy taffy to the famous sweetgrass baskets that Gulla women have been weaving for generations.
10 a.m.-dusk.

drive

From Charleston, Kiawah Island is less than an hour. But you'll definitely want to stop at one of the large plantations sprinkled around the downtown area. Magnolia's internationally famous gardens are America's oldest (circa 1676). Take Calhoun Street to the Robert B. Scarborough Bridge, then merge onto Highway 61 toward Summerville before taking a slight left at Ashley River Road. After a couple of miles, you'll take a right at Savage Road and then continue on Ashley River Road for nearly six miles. This will give you a chance to see some of the rural communities surrounding the downtown area. When you pull into Magnolia, you'll have to pass through a set of gates. Here's where you have to decide which tours you want to purchase, so be ready (definitely see the gardens, the rest depends on how much time you have).

Magnolia Plantation • Fort Sumter • Nathaniel Russell House Staircase • Nathaniel Russell House

see

Magnolia Plantation and Gardens

3550 Ashley River Road, Charleston, 843-571-1266, 800-367-3517; www.magnoliaplantation.com

Incredibly, this plantation is still managed by the same family. Eleven generations of Draytons have lovingly attended to this magical place since 1676. The gardens cover 50 acres with camellias, azaleas, magnolias and hundreds of other flowering species. Tour the classic Southern home, which has a great collection of early American antiques; hike the nature trail (where you're likely to spot alligators, turtles, herons and more) or take a boat ride through the canals of the former rice fields and the Ashley River. The plantation itself includes more than 500 acres. Canoe and bicycle rentals are available. March-October 8 a.m.-dusk, November-February call for hours. Gardens only: $15

drive

Leaving Magnolia, head southeast on Ashley River Road for a little more than two miles and then turn right on Bees Ferry Road. After that it's left at Main, which turns into Bohicket Road, which you'll be on for seven miles. Most of this is two-lane road hugged by oaks with their canopy of Spanish moss. If you're driving in the afternoon, you'll catch the sun's rays darting through. Along the way, you'll pass through quiet communities with tiny churches and horse farms. After a while, the road opens up and you'll be

**KIAWAH ISLAND
GOLF COURSE**

on Betsy Kerrison Parkway. When you see the traffic circle, take the third exit onto Kiawah Island Parkway and then make a right at Surf Watch Drive and then an immediate left at Eugenia Avenue.

stop

After a couple of days of rollicking in Charleston, Kiawah Island is the perfect place to relax. Named for the Native Americans who once hunted and fished here, the island is separated from the mainland by the Kiawah River and a mile-wide salt marsh, and is one of the richest natural environments on the eastern seaboard. Separate resort areas and private residential neighborhoods ensure a minimum of traffic and leave much of the island untouched. On Kiawah, sunny days are filled with great golf, good food and happy outdoor fun. The accommodations are top-notch and the tennis and golf are world-class (scores of tournaments have taken place here, including the Ryder Cup). There's also 10 miles of glorious white-sand beach that some say is the best anywhere, and we have to agree. Rent a bike and cruise around the island, taking in the ocean breezes and the beautiful homes. You'll find many tours to explore the wildlife.

stay

★★★★★The Sanctuary Hotel at Kiawah Island
1 Sanctuary Beach Drive, Kiawah Island, 843-768-6000, 877-683-1234; www.thesanctuary.com
This grand resort resembling an old Southern estate is the place to stay on Kiawah Island, thanks to its spectacular beachfront setting, fine dining and first-class spa. The gorgeous lobby with creaky walnut floors and handcrafted rugs is set up like a wealthy great aunt's living room, with intimate seating areas, limestone fireplaces and wood cabinets full of porcelain knickknacks. Large windows look out to the perfectly manicured lawns and the beach right beyond. Two large staircases and murals depicting the island's wildlife flank the elegant space. Rooms (be sure to ask for an ocean view) have a breezy traditional feel with their early American furniture, four-poster beds, large tubs, colorful drapes and plantation shutters. The café next to the pool is a great spot for lunch, and the lounge off the lobby is perfect for a cocktail after a day on the golf course.

THE LOBBY BAR AT THE SANCTUARY

Throw in some Southern hospitality, which they do, and you won't want to leave.

255 rooms. Wireless Internet access. Three restaurants, three bars. Children's activity center. Airport transportation available. Fitness center. Tennis. Beach. Pool. Spa. Business center. $$$$

eat

★★★★Ocean Room

1 Sanctuary Beach Drive, Kiawah Island, 843-768-6253, 877-683-1234;
www.thesanctuary.com

The staff at this elegant restaurant charms guests while serving up seasonal New American dishes such as seared Hudson Valley foie gras with sautéed snow peas, sweet soy and snow pea sorbet, or seared rare Ahi tuna with crispy shrimp dumplings, wilted wasabi leaves and lavender-scented jasmine rice. You can also sit at the bar and order from the snack menu with items like the braised short ribs egg rolls and caramel fondue for dessert. You'll find wines here that aren't available anywhere else.

Seafood menu. Dinner. Bar. Resort formal, jackets preferred. Reservations recommended. $$$

The Atlantic Room

At the Ocean Course Clubhouse

Time your reservation with the sunset—the Atlantic Room has great views of the coast. The satisfying menu includes steakhouse classics, seafood and divine desserts, all of which are more thoroughly enjoyed with a bottle from the nice selection of wines.

Steak, American menu. Breakfast, lunch, dinner. Bar. Children's menu. Casual attire. Reservations recommended. $$$

Osprey Point Grill

At Osprey Point Golf Club

This casual grill room and bar offers great views of Osprey Point Golf Course and is the perfect place to start and finish your day of golf. Stop in

before your game—the chefs will box up your breakfast for you or serve it outside on the veranda. After your game, tally up your score with a juicy burger and a cold one.
American menu. Breakfast, lunch. $$

Turtle Point Bar & Grill
At Turtle Point Golf Club
You can get everything from grilled steaks to wings at this all-American bar and grill. The comfortable leather chairs and televisions invite you to sit back for hours. A golfer's breakfast buffet is served each morning.
American menu. Lunch, dinner. $$

Kiawah Island Beach • Pool at The Sanctuary • The Sanctuary • Wildlife on Kiawah Island

spa

★★★★★Spa at The Sanctuary
1 Sanctuary Beach Drive, Kiawah Island, 843-768-6340;
www.thesanctuary.com
Located inside the Sanctuary, the Spa resembles a grand seaside mansion. The hospitable staff greet guests with herbal tea and fresh fruit before leading the way to one of 12 rooms for nature-based treatments, which feature botanical extracts and natural enzymes. The low country verbena body polish uses fresh lemon verbena and mild buffing grains of ruby grapefruit and blood orange extracts to hydrate skin. The exercise facility features the latest cardiovascular and resistance equipment, a 65-foot-long indoor pool and Pilates and yoga studios.

see

Bike riding
843-768-6005
The best way to get around the island is on a bike. There are more than 30 miles of trails and 10 miles of beach. Pick up a bike at one of three locations: West Beach Bike Shop, Night Heron Park Nature Center and the Sanctuary. There are half-day, full-day, three-day and weekly rates.

Golf
If you love golf, you've found nirvana. The island is home to five championship golf courses designed by the world's leading architects, including the Pete Dye-designed Ocean Course, which will host the PGA Championship

THE SUN SETS ON KIAWAH ISLAND

in 2012. Greens fees for Ocean range from $239 to $320; the other courses start at $85 and go up to $215, including a cart.

Kayaking

Go kayaking through Kiawah's lazy salt marshes and check out the wildlife, including river otters and osprey. Twilight trips are also available. Or sign up for a surf kayak, where an instructor takes you out to experience the best low country "white water."

Tennis

West Beach Village, East Beach Village (across from the Two Center), 843-768-2838
Kiawah Island has some of the best tennis around. You'll find 23 Har Tru courts split between two locations, plus lighted hard courts and a myriad of activities. Sign up for match making or the adult doubles round robin. The stroke-a-day clinic allows you to learn about one specific stroke in each one-hour session.

Walking tours

Take a nature tour to see the alligators (naturalists will explain why there are so many on Kiawah) or explore the island's other wildlife. Night beach walks will tell you everything you wanted to know about sea turtles and other nocturnal animals that live on the beach. You can also go beach combing or on a garden tour of the Sanctuary.

drive

The drive back to Savannah will take about two and a half hours. This route includes a stop in Beaufort. Leaving Kiawah, head back to Bohicket Road, which will turn into Main. Turn left at the Savannah Highway and go for 20 miles. After that, continue for a bit on Ace Basin Parkway (a pretty stretch) and then hop back onto US-17 heading south. The last trek is on Highway 21 South, where you'll stay for nearly 15 miles until you get to Beaufort.

THE MORNING ROOM AT
THE SANCTUARY

THE OCEAN ROOM AT
THE SANCTUARY

stop

The second oldest town in the state, Beaufort is the
unofficial capital of South Carolina's low country,
and is filled with antebellum homes and churches.
The town has rebuilt itself several times, first after
Native Americans destroyed it in 1715, then after
the British attacked in 1812 and finally after Union
troops forced the evacuation of almost the entire
town during the Civil War. Tidy Victorian houses and
a small set of storefronts and restaurants overlook a
beautiful marshland landscape. Stop in **Plum's** (*904
1/2 Bay St., Beaufort, 843-525-1946; www.plums
restaurant.com*) for a casual bite out on the back
porch overlooking Waterfront Park and the Beaufort River. The restaurant offers fresh salads and
satisfying sandwiches (try the turkey with brie and
strawberry jam). On your way out, be sure to get
an ice cream to enjoy on your stroll through town.
The story is that Barbra Streisand often came here
for ice cream when she was filming *Prince of Tides*
and always ordered the coffee almond fudge. The
flavor is now named after the movie, and really is
delicious.

drive

After Beaufort, you'll only have an hour back to
Savannah. Head north on Highway 21 and then
take Highway 170. After about 30 miles, you'll get
on Highway 17 for the last leg back into Savannah.
Your trip may be over, but your lovely weekend
won't soon be forgotten.

CHAPTER 12
SEATTLE TO VANCOUVER

The 141-mile trip from Seattle to Vancouver across the border is a spectacular way to explore the Pacific Northwest. The scenic drive up Route 5 hugs the coast and makes the two-and-a-half hour journey nearly as enjoyable as the destination itself. The beautiful city of Vancouver is full of wonderful surprises, from great shopping that rivals New York to the diverse cuisine (with plenty of fresh catch) to the vibrant arts scene. From here, you can also easily make the trip up to Whistler, site of the 2010 Winter Olympic Games, for its spectacular ski slopes and beautiful winter scenery. The summer also boasts gorgeous vistas of the Canadian Rockies and a myriad of outdoor activities. While snow is rare in Seattle, the Northwest does have a substantial rainy season from November to January that tapers off into spring. (Temperatures during winter months are typically in the 40s and 50s.) But don't let that deter you. This trip can be enjoyed year-round. Just don't forget your passport.

Whistler

LION'S GATE
BRIDGE

99

Granville
Island

Vancouver

VANCOUVER
AQUARIUM

CANADA

U.S.A.

VANCOUVER
ISLAND

5

Seattle

SPACE NEEDLE

N
W   E
S

starting out

The Mobil Four-Star **Fairmont Olympic Hotel** (*411 University St., Seattle, 206-621-1700, 800-257-7544; www.fairmont.com*) is conveniently located in Rainier Square, only minutes from Seattle's top attractions.

drive

Grab a coffee and leave the Space Needle behind as you begin your drive to the westernmost Canadian province, British Columbia. Pick up Seattle's Interstate 5 (the major north-south expressway in the city) and head north. The drive mainly runs alongside a series of inlets, bays and peninsulas that separate the U.S. mainland from Victoria, the capitol of B.C., but you'll have to wander to the west of I-5 to a series of smaller roads if you really want to explore. It may take up to 30 minutes to overcome the Seattle city limits, but soon the scenery will become more rural as the urban traffic tapers off, allowing most drivers to make it from Seattle to the border in an hour and a half. The Peace Arch Park will be your last landmark on the U.S. side of the border and makes for a perfect photo opportunity and a great place to get out and stretch your legs. Depending on the time of day, lengthy lines at the

The Sutton Place Hotel Wine Merchant ▪ Pool at Four Seasons Vancouver ▪ Dining room at Four Seasons Vancouver ▪ Grand Suite at The Sutton Place Hotel

border crossing can add to your drive time; your best bet is to try to make it to the border by mid-morning or late in the evening to hit the shortest lines. Also, when crossing into Canada, you might hit some construction as the border crossing is being rebuilt for the arrival of the 2010 Winter Olympics.

After you cross the border, it's only another 45 minutes to Vancouver. Remain on I-5 (which becomes Highway 99 North at the border) and keep your eyes out for the Vancouver International Airport. Cross the Arthur Lang Bridge and follow signs to take Granville Street north. This route will take you through some lovely residential areas as well as through the trendy South Granville neighborhood, which is an absolute must-see for shopping aficionados. As you approach Granville Bridge, you will have the perfect vantage point for a beautiful panorama of Vancouver, and on a clear day, a full view of the Canadian Rockies as well. Cross the bridge over False Creek and you'll have landed yourself in the heart of the city. If you can stave off those shopping urges, head straight to your hotel to check in and ditch your wheels, as this British Columbian paradise is best explored on foot.

FOUR SEASONS VANCOUVER

stop

The city of Vancouver is all about impressive threes: It's the third biggest city in Canada; boasts the third largest film production industry in North America (awarding it the nickname "Hollywood North"); and is consistently ranked one of the three most livable cities in the world. The first major settlement took place in the 1860s by immigrants looking for gold, and Vancouver reaped the benefits of the creation of the transcontinental railroad and transformed from a small lumber town to the busiest seaport in Canada today.

Offering year-round activities for outdoor enthusiasts, the city provides a little bit of everything, and people are starting to take notice. With tourism booming, gourmet restaurants popping up by the dozen and great shopping, it's a must-see metropolis.

stay

★★★★The Sutton Place Hotel

845 Burrard St., Vancouver, 604-682-5511, 866-378-8866;
www.suttonplace.com

Located in the business and shopping core of downtown Vancouver, the hotel offers guest rooms that exude a European flavor, while the dining and lounge areas feature comforting Old-World motifs. The hotel also offers a serene spa, indoor swimming pool under a big sunroof, and a fitness center. Treat yourself to the luxurious Vida Wellness Spa—a Thai massage, perhaps—to release any stress from the days' drive.

372 rooms. Wireless Internet access. Two restaurants, bar. Fitness center. Pool. Spa. Business center. Pets accepted. $$$

★★★★Four Seasons Hotel Vancouver

791 W. Georgia St., Vancouver, 604-689-9333; www.fourseasons.com/vancouver

Located downtown in the commercial and cultural hub of the city, the Four Seasons Hotel Vancouver is connected via the lobby to the underground Pacific Centre Mall, so you don't even need an umbrella to go shopping during the rainy Pacific Northwest winter. A mere block from Robson Street, a favorite shopping and strolling spot for Vancouverites and visitors alike, the Four Seasons is also adjacent to the Vancouver Art Gallery and a 10-minute walk to Coal Harbour's cafés and restaurants, with that peninsular paradise known as Stanley Park a little farther along. When making a reservation, request a room on an upper floor facing north and you'll wake up to an awesome alpine panorama (on a clear day). Also great for families, the hotel features an indoor/outdoor pool, in-room PlayStations, and a selection of board games available from the concierge, as well as family-friendly menu items at the hotel's two restaurants.

376 rooms. High-speed Internet access. Two restaurants, bar. Fitness center. Pool. Business center. Pets accepted. $$$

eat

If you're lucky enough to be pulling into Vancouver around lunchtime, the options are plentiful, from a quick bite to a full epicurean affair. For those eager to get going around the city, opt for a tasty—yet speedy—lunch in the Kitsilano neighborhood. **Trafalgars Bistro** (*2603 W. 16th Ave., 604-739-0555; www.trafalgars.com*) is a wonderful off-the-beaten-path spot offering outdoor seating (weather permitting) and plenty of gourmet takes on familiar menu selections. An artichoke and tomato grilled cheese on rosemary sourdough or lamb cheeseburger make for a tough lunch decision. Be sure to stop next door and satisfy your sweet tooth at **Sweet Obsession** (*2611 W. 16th Ave., 604-739-0555; www.sweetobsession.ca*) where you'll find dozens of homemade cake, flan and tart varieties. Vancouver also has several wonderful fine dining restaurants, including:

★★★★La Belle Auberge
4856 48th Ave., Ladner, 604-946-7717;
www.labelleauberge.com
If you crave the glorious food of France's best kitchens, opt for a 30-minute drive from Vancouver to Ladner and enjoy dinner at La Belle Auberge. Set in a charming early 1900s country inn, the restaurant houses five antiques-filled salon-style dining rooms. The kitchen, led by chef/owner Bruno Marti, a masterful culinary technician, offers spectacular, authentic French cuisine.

French menu. Dinner. Closed Sunday-Monday; also two weeks in January. Business casual attire. Reservations recommended. Outdoor seating. $$$

A SWEET OBSESSION CAKE

WEST

LUMIERE

★★★★Lumiere

2551 W. Broadway, Vancouver, 604-739-8185;
www.lumiere.ca

Lumiere is a stunning and elegant restaurant that offers European-style dining of the most divine order. The inspired and innovative fare is French with Asian accents and displays a respect for regional ingredients. While the eight-course menu could be overkill, each portion is perfectly sized so that you don't finish dinner feeling perilously inflated. Instead, you feel deliciously satiated and utterly pampered by the experience. The global wine list is in sync with the kitchen's style, but attention should also be paid to the classic cocktails served at Lumiere's sexy bar. The bartenders here follow a pre-Prohibition style, where the craft of the cocktail is taken as seriously as the mastery of the plate.

French menu. Dinner. Closed Monday. Bar. Business casual attire. Reservations recommended. Valet parking. Outdoor seating. $$$$

★★★★Bishop's

2183 W. Fourth Ave., Vancouver, 604-738-2025;
www.bishopsonline.com

Intimate, modern and airy, with a loft-like yet upscale feel, this chic duplex restaurant is known for West Coast continental cuisine and has a menu that emphasizes seasonal, organic produce and locally sourced seafood. It isn't uncommon to spy celebrities and VIPs nibbling on these delicious culinary wares. For those who like to sample lots of different wines with dinner, Bishop's offers a nice selection of wines by the glass and an outstanding range of wines by the half-bottle. In addition to being a visionary chef, owner John Bishop is a gracious host.

International menu. Dinner. Closed first week in January. Bar. Business casual attire. Reservations recommended. Outdoor seating. $$$

★★★★West

2881 Granville St., Vancouver, 604-738-8938; www.westrestaurant.com

West is one of those sleek spots that makes sipping cocktails for hours on end an easy task. It is an ideal choice for gourmets in search of an inventive, eclectic meal, as well as those who crave local flavor and seasonal ingredients. Located in Vancouver's chic South Granville neighborhood, West offers diners the chance to sample the vibrant cuisine of the Pacific Northwest region. Stunning, locally sourced ingredients are on display here thanks to the masterful kitchen. International menu. Lunch, dinner. Bar. Business casual attire. Reservations recommended. Valet parking. $$$

shop

From Maple leaf key chains to Cartier clasps, Vancouver proudly considers itself Canada's shopping hub. And because the city comprises a cluster of neighborhoods, different areas cater to different tastes and styles, and almost all of them are within walking distance of the city center.

Heritage District

Find your way to the intersection of Howe and Hastings Streets, and you will be surrounded by luxury brands such as Cartier, Dunhill, Hugo Boss and a store called **Leone** (757 W. Hastings St., 604-683-1133; www. leone.ca), which carries the likes of Versace and Escada. A little further east, at the intersection of Granville and Dunsmuir, just around the corner from the Four Seasons Vancouver, check out the newly redesigned flagship **Holt Renfrew** (Pacific Centre, 737 Dunsmuir St., 604-681-3121; www.holtrenfrew.com). This is the Canadian version of Bloomingdale's and Neiman Marcus—combined—a definite stop for any diehard shopper. Right up the street at the historic Fairmont Hotel, you'll find the luxury retailers Louis Vuitton, Hermès, Tiffany and Coach.

Robson Street between Burrard and Jervis

www.robsonstreet.ca
Vancouver's most famous shopping street, Robson features block after block of neighborhood shopping with coffee shops, restaurants and cafes mixed in. Stores run the gamut from Ferragamo to Roots and Zara. Weekends and evenings bring street performers and live outdoor entertainment to this popular shopping strip.

South Granville

2300 Granville St., Vancouver, www.southgranville.org
If it's boutique shopping you're after, head to the South Granville neighborhood. Tucked among galleries and teashops, upscale names like Max Mara, DKNY and Williams-Sonoma mix fitfully with unique local shops such as **Country Furniture** (3097 Loranville St., Vancouver, 604-738-6411; www.countryfurniture. net), **Farmhouse** (2915 Granville St., Vancouver, 604-738-0167; www. farmhousecollections.com) and **Lothantique** (2655 South Granville St., Vancouver, 604-738-4888; www.lothantiquevancouver.com) for skincare products. First established with the carriage trade in the 1920s, South Granville has burgeoned into the home of more than 200 stores, restaurants and galleries. Be sure to stop for a little chocolate pick-me-up at either **Daniel le Chocolat Belge** or **Purdy's**, both located on Granville Street. Within this neighborhood you'll also find Gallery Row, which is home to more than 30 galleries and antiques stores. Be sure to check out the **Douglas Reynolds Gallery** (2335 Granville St., Vancouver, 604-731-9292; www.douglasreynolds gallery.com) for its amazing selection of museum-quality Northwest coast native art and jewelry.

VANCOUVER ART GALLERY

Yaletown

www.myyaletown.com

Yet another shopping and dining destination, Yaletown is situated near the water's edge of downtown Vancouver. A unique warehouse district neighborhood, Yaletown is filled with restaurants and cafés, home design shops and galleries.

see

Stanley Park

North foot of Georgia St., Vancouver; www.vancouver.ca/parks/parks/stanley

You'll want to devote an entire morning or afternoon at the 1,000-acre Stanley Park (wear good walking shoes). Located at the western edge of the city, the lush park is home to the city's aquarium and a variety of walking and hiking trails that give you a bird's-eye view of the city, the mountains and the ocean. It's also famous for its seawall, perfect for catching ocean views and photo opportunities. A morning or afternoon can also be spent perusing Stanley Park's ample gardens; the Ted and Mary Greig Rhododendron Garden features thousands of the bright blossoms while floral display beds within the park host many rose varieties amounting to some 3,500 plants. (Stanley Park was, in its infancy, home to a cornucopia of rose species that grew in the many greenhouses that once stood here.) Walk along the seawall to get some of the best views, as it stretches a full 8.8 kilometers (5.5 miles) around the edge of the park. Take note of monuments and plaques along the seawall and throughout Stanley Park; many mark historic events and important Canucks, including a series of totem poles at Brockton Point recognizing the early human habitation of the Vancouver area.

Vancouver Art Gallery

Hornby and Robson Streets, Vancouver, 604-662-4719; www.vanartgallery.bc.ca

Located in the heart of the city, this gallery offers visitors access to a vast collection of contemporary artwork featuring a host of internationally recognized artists from British Columbia as well as one of the most extensive collections of native Emily Carr's work. The permanent collection has nearly

10,000 pieces in its inventory and exhibits range from solo artists to traveling exhibitions and theme collections. Daily 10 a.m.-5:30 p.m., Tuesday and Thursday 10 a.m.-9 p.m.

Vancouver Aquarium Marine Science Centre

845 Avision Way, Vancouver, 604-659-3474; www.vanaqua.org

Located within Stanley Park, the Vancouver Aquarium is Canada's largest aquarium. From Beluga whales to sea otters, dolphins and sharks, this facility has it all, and offers plenty of daily hands-on activities and information sessions. Daily: winter 9:30 a.m.-5 p.m., summer 9:30 a.m.-7 p.m.

Granville Island

Anderson and Cartwright Streets, Vancouver, 604-666-5784; www.granvilleisland.bc.ca

JELLYFISH AT VANCOUVER AQUARIUM

Visit this small island within the city to explore the work of a variety of artists, as well as galleries, an expansive daily public market (with local produce including giant fresh strawberries), shops, restaurants, theaters and a working art school—all housed in unique tin factory-style buildings. Take the Aquabus or False Creek Ferry from downtown to save the hassle of finding a parking spot as parking on the island is limited. Daily 9 a.m.-7 p.m.

drive

While you still have room in your trunk, bid your farewells to Vancouver and head north. Whistler Blackcomb Village is the place to extend your stay in British Columbia, if for nothing else than the drive up along the coast. One of the most beautiful and scenic drives the northwest has to offer, it takes just an hour and a half from Vancouver along the Sea-to-Sky Highway. Follow signs to Highway 99—the road literally hugs the coastline past Bowen, Gambier and Anvil islands before cutting back into the mainland and mountain terrain north into Whistler. As you leave Vancouver, you'll drive back through Stanley Park, where the majestic pines tower effortlessly over the road. Cross Lions Gate Bridge, spanning high above the Burrard Inlet and keep your eyes peeled for seaplanes landing and refueling at the unique floating gas stations. Continue out of the city into North Vancouver and have your camera ready—designated lookout sites offer panoramic views along the majestic Rockies and waterways. Look for signs for Shannon Falls; a short hike affords access to a spectacular waterfall and is well worth the stop.

FOUR SEASONS RESORT WHISTLER

Your journey follows Howe Sound (a glacially formed fjord) up to dramatic vistas of British Columbia's Coastal Range and the eternal snows that cap their peaks.

stop

More than two million visitors come to Whistler each year, primarily for the 200-plus ski trails and some three-dozen lifts on its two peaks (Whistler being one, Blackcomb the other). Whistler boasts an average annual snowfall of more than 400 inches. But there's more to Whistler than mere mountain sports.

When you arrive in the ski town of Whistler, pass by the recently developed Creekside Village, and soon you will reach the Whistler Blackcomb Village—a dining and lodging destination that has won numerous design awards and provides a peerless getaway for luxury travelers from Canada, the U.S. and beyond. A relatively untapped wilderness till 1962 when four businessmen began looking into constructing a ski resort to make a bid for the 1968 Winter Olympics, Whistler has always awed people by its natural beauty. Views surround every peak and the small-town feel makes it a perfect weekend detour.

Summer kayaking in Whistler • Scenic winter views • Whistler Blackcomb Village • Four Seasons Whistler

stay

★★★★Four Seasons Resort Whistler

4591 Blackcomb Way, Whistler, 604-935-3400; www.fourseasons.com/whistler
This resort is far enough from the village center for secluded serenity, yet close enough to get to by foot. Some of the best ski slopes on the continent are right outside the door of this luxury hotel. The style here is rustic modern—a brilliant blend of West Coast, European and Asian influences, featuring natural local greystone, artistically combined with polished woods. A stunning sculpted metal screen of delicate interwoven tree branches, reminiscent of the nearby forest, separates the small lobby (on the second floor) from the staircase down to the bistro/bar, shops and meeting rooms. If you venture to Whistler in winter, look forward to the outdoor fireside s'mores and hot chocolate poolside (the heated pools are open year round). For real luxury in this mountainside retreat, book a few treatments at the Spa at the Four Seasons; the Sea to Sky body treatment is a unique experience that uses ingredients indigenous to the Canadian west coast.

ARAXI

273 rooms. High-speed Internet access. Restaurant, bar. Children's activity center. Fitness center. Pool. Airport transportation available. Spa. Business center. Pets accepted. $$$$

eat

★★★Araxi

4222 Village Square, Whistler, 604-932-4540; www.araxi.com

Original artworks and antiques adorn the warm and friendly dining room at Araxi. French and Italian culinary styles influence the cuisine that is largely made from fine, regional ingredients. Visit the raw bar for an appetizer and cocktail before diving into the main dining experience.

Pacific Northwest menu. Lunch, dinner. Closed two weeks in early May and late October. Bar. Business casual attire. Reservations recommended. Outdoor seating. $$$

★★★Bearfoot Bistro

4121 Village Green, Whistler, 604-932-3433; www.bearfootbistro.com

Bistro almost seems like a misnomer for this tasting mecca that is the perfect end to a day of relaxing on Blackcomb Mountain. Set aside some time to enjoy each of five courses on the chef's menu, which are handcrafted from a huge range of rare, high-quality ingredients, including caribou and pheasant. Or create your own three-course menu (suggested wine pairings available). Add to this one of the most beautiful locations in North America and the result is a truly standout dining experience.

International menu. Dinner. Bar. Business casual attire. Reservations recommended. Valet parking. $$$$

drive

The drive home is a simple one: Highway 99 (Sea-to-Sky Highway) goes directly south to Seattle. Again, plan to avoid peak border traffic times, if possible, and remember that once you cross into Washington State, the highway turns into Interstate 5.

INN AT
LITTLE WASHINGTON
N
W
E
S
Washington, D.C.
66
15
211
Washington
Amissville
UNICORN WINERY
WASHINGTON
MONUMENT
SHENANDOAH NATIONAL PARK

CHAPTER 13
WASHINGTON TO WASHINGTON

The capital city is always buzzing with the business of running our nation, but what many people may not know (even Washingtonians themselves) is that there's another Washington—one that moves at a slower pace, a place more connected to the countryside and nature, where you can unwind and reflect. And where someone will take care of your every need. This other Washington is only 67 miles from D.C. in the heart of the Virginia horse country and the bucolic landscape that abuts the Appalachian Mountains. Often referred to as Little Washington, the town is home to a year-round dream getaway—the fabulous Inn at Little Washington. Here you'll find sumptuous accommodations, one of the best restaurants in the world and an unparalleled level of customer service where you can truly leave your cares behind.

WASHINGTON
MONUMENT

THE INN AT LITTLE
WASHINGTON

starting out

If you're from out of town and haven't seen the sites in a while, book a stay at the Mobil Five-Star **Four Seasons Hotel** (*2800 Pennsylvania Ave., N.W., Washington D.C., 202-342-0444, 800-332-3442; www. fourseasons.com*). Located in historic Georgetown, the hotel delivers a refined residential experience that extends from your first step into the modern, sophisticated lobby to lights out in one of the luxuriously appointed guest rooms.

drive

The actual journey toward your weekend retreat begins by heading west on Constitution Avenue a few blocks and merging onto Interstate 66 West. This main corridor out of the city crosses the Potomac River and passes below the town of Rosslyn. Here, densely packed and sleek high-rise buildings seem out of place after the openness of both terrain and sky of the National Mall. During rush hour, and up to an hour afterward, I-66 will slow to a crawl at a few choke points during the first 10 miles to the Capital Beltway. Still, it's the most efficient and convenient way out of town. Speed picks up after the Beltway with only occasional traffic jams when there's construction, an accident or bad weather.

Continue on I-66 for another three miles to Haymarket and follow exit 40 onto Route 15 South. You've arrived in Virginia Horse Country. After crossing Route 55, stop to smell the leather at Saddlery Liquidators. Turn left at the store's sign and then weave in behind a farm supply warehouse to find the entrance.

see

Saddlery Liquidators
6612 James Madison Highway, Haymarket,
888-723-3554
From saddles to boots to polo equipment, this store holds over 24,000 square feet of discounted equestrian supplies. A horse lover could easily spend hours browsing the aisles. Monday-Saturday 10 a.m.-6 p.m., Sunday 11 a.m.-4 p.m.

drive

Continuing south, the two lane road is embraced on both sides by tall trees and joins Route 29 after four miles. Turn right and follow Route 29 South up and down rolling hills where farms, country stores, nurseries and unique shops line both sides of the road. There are Amish sheds and barns, chainsaw sculptures and often signs indicating that bulls are for sale. At nine miles, turn right on Business Route 29 into Warrenton. Suburban sprawl reappears on this short stretch. Go to the fourth traffic light and turn left onto Main Street. Up a hill you'll leave behind the chain stores and discover one of Virginia's many historic small towns. The Fauquier County Seat retains the charm of its courthouse roots. Red brick buildings dating back to the 19th century house antiques shops, galleries, specialty boutiques, cafés and restaurants. Parking is available on the street and in lots that are well marked. For lunch, stop in at **Molly's Irish Pub** (*36 Main St., Warrenton, 540-349-5300; www.mollysirishpub.com; daily 11 a.m.-11 p.m.*) The tavern serves the usual "pub grub," such as fish and chips, bangers and mash, onion rings and Irish stew. The extensive menu also includes salmon fillet and grilled cod. Of course, there is a wide selection of beers, a dozen on tap and a selection of 40 bottled beers.

Backtrack down Main Street and turn left and then right onto Route 211 West. The sky opens and the Blue Ridge Mountains appear in the distance. The mountains get their name from the blue color of the dark and hazy forest and its reflection against the sky. This section of Route 211 remains one of the most scenic sections of road in the state. The four-lane road follows the foothills and valleys with farms and green pastures on both sides. All the while the peaks of Shenandoah National Park grow taller. Horse fences border the road and long driveways lead to country estates. You can almost smell the old money of the landed gentry. Throughout Virginia signs featuring a cluster of grapes indicate nearby vineyards. After seven miles, turn right at one of these signs onto Old Bridge Road, and proceed 2.5 miles for some wine tasting.

THE INN AT LITTLE WASHINGTON

FOLIAGE IN WASHINGTON

see

Unicorn Winery

89 Old Bridge Road, Amissville, 540-349-5885, www.unicornwinery.com
The winery makes more than a dozen wines. The spacious tasting room
also includes two outside decks overlooking rows of grapevines and a
large koi and lily pond. The tasting fee is $5. Monday-Friday noon-5 p.m.,
Saturday-Sunday 11 a.m.-5 p.m.

Gray Ghost Vineyards

14706 Lee Highway, Amissville, 540-937-4869; www.grayghostvineyards.com
Return to Route 211 West and proceed another four miles for more wine
at Gray Ghost Vineyards on the left. Named after the local Confederate
Colonel John S. Mosby, who received the nickname Gray Ghost from the
Union Army for his ability to infiltrate enemy lines undetected, the winery offers free tastings (on selected dates) in a cathedral-like space with 25-foot
ceilings, a balcony and a bar that seems to stretch to infinity. The building
also houses a second tasting room upstairs and a separate hall for special
winemaker's dinners. In addition to the usual chardonnay and cabernet
sauvignon, they serve a vidal blanc and a gewürztraminer. Gray Ghost also
makes adieu, a delicious dessert wine.
Friday-Sunday 11 a.m.-5 p.m., January-February Saturday-Sunday 11
a.m.-5 p.m.

*Gifts at R.H. Ballard • Lucky Duck dish at the Inn at Little Washington • The Inn at Little
Washington veranda (right) and guest room*

drive

Follow Route 211 for 12 more miles of superb scenery and turn right onto
Route 211 Business West. Pass an old stone wall on the right and arrive at
the inn after a half mile. Pull up under the four flags adorning the Inn at Little Washington for valet parking or park in the church lot across the street.

stop

The town of Washington, Virginia is small—very, very small. A brisk walk
around town takes less than 10 minutes. The inn dominates the city with
its gallery and shops, which features tableware, gifts, antiques and jewelry.
Hand-made gold and silver jewelry is also available at **Goodine's Designs
in Gold and Silver**, (*353 Main St., Washington, 540-675-3190, Thursday-*

THE INN AT LITTLE WASHINGTON

Monday 10 a.m.-6 p.m., Wednesday 3-6 p.m.). At **R.H. Ballard Art Rug and Home** (*307 Main St., Washington, 540-675-1411; www.rhballard.com; daily 10 a.m.-6 p.m.*), find an eclectic mix of Oriental rugs, fine art, tablecloths and purses. The town also includes several other galleries and two theaters.

stay

★★★★★The Inn at Little Washington
309 Main St., Washington, 540-675-3800; www.theinnatlittlewashington.com
Except for the flags, the inn seems unassuming from the outside, re-sembling a simple turn-of-the-century building. The building, in fact, was formerly a gas station. But once inside you'll find an enclave of quiet luxury. The cozy lobby looks like a set of a turn-of-the-century film, while at the same time feeling like a European country inn. The walls are adorned with rich fabrics and deep colors—the ceilings ornate. There are comfortable upholstered furnishings, antiques, portraits, sculptures and busts, a grand gilded mirror and a fireplace. It's hard to nail down the décor as any one style. Every square inch appears to have been painstakingly planned— which happens to be the case. The inn was and is decorated by London stage set designer Joyce Evans in collaboration with the inn's owner and chef, Patrick O'Connell. Whatever one might call it, the interior is inviting. You just want to plop down in a chair and look around the room. The inn has 18 rooms and suites, each uniquely decorated, plus two separate cot-tages. The well-trained staff are ready to take care of any and all needs— from packing a picnic to drawing out a route for a scenic drive to making reservations for any activity or being available to serve tea or wine if you wish to do nothing at all.
18 rooms. Closed Tuesday in January-March and July. Complimentary continental breakfast. Restaurant, bar. $$$$

THE PORCH AT THE INN AT
LITTLE WASHINGTON

eat

★★★★★The Inn at Little Washington

The inn is perhaps most famous for its restaurant.
Chef Patrick O'Connell has amassed almost every
culinary award in existence. Diners will see why.
Seasonal dishes include a crab cake "sandwich"
with fried green tomatoes and tomato vinaigrette,
sesame-crusted Chilean sea bass with baby shrimp,
artichokes and grape tomatoes, rabbit braised in
apple cider with wild mushrooms and garlic mashed
potatoes, and for dessert, pistachio and white
chocolate ice cream terrine with blackberry sauce.
The multi-hour meal is definitely worth a visit. Meanwhile, the service is like nowhere else. When diners
arrive, their mood is given a rating of one to 10 by
the waitstaff. It's a secret that isn't revealed to the
diner. If you've had a bad day or are just in a lousy
mood, you may receive a lower rating. The goal of
the waitstaff is to insure that you are at least at a
nine by the end of dinner.
American menu. Dinner. Closed Tuesday (except
in May and October). Bar. Business casual attire.
Reservations recommended. Valet parking. $$$$

see

Ballooning

*Blue Ride Hot Air Balloons, Front Royal, 540-622-6325;
www.rideair.com*
Perhaps the best way to enjoy the Blue Ride is from
above, in a hot air balloon. Flights take off first thing
in the morning or at the end of the day when winds
are light. An average flight lasts just over an hour
and ends with a champagne toast, a tradition that
began in 18th-century France. A glass of bubbly,
however, is just icing on the cake. A balloon will take
you up to heights of several thousand feet to witness a panoramic view of the Virginia countryside.
But a hot air balloon can also descend and skim just
above the treetops as it rides with the wind. Soaring
birds, such as hawks and eagles, often investigate
the colorful bulbous creature and join you in flight.
$200 per person.

A DOLLOP OF OSETRA
CAVIAR FROM THE INN AT
LITTLE WASHINGTON

Canoeing/Kayaking

Shenandoah River Outfitters (*6502 S. Page Valley Road, Luray, 540-743-4159; www.shenandoahriver.com*) offers a variety of canoeing and kayaking trips on the Shenandoah River. The river flows between the Massanutten Ridge and the Blue Ridge of Shenandoah National Park and is considered to be the most scenic section of the river. Wherever you go, you always have a view of the mountains. One-day trips include a beginner 1.5-hour flat-water paddle and a five-hour trip that includes a taste of the rapids and whitewater. Two- and three-day canoeing and camping trips are also available. If you don't want to paddle, try tubing. Just sit back and enjoy gentle rapids and fantastic scenery on this 3- to 4-hour float. Shenandoah River Outfitters also rents canoes and kayaks. **Front Royal Canoe** (*8567 Stonewall Jackson Highway, Front Royal, 540-635-5440; www.frontroyalcanoe. com*) operates a variety of canoe, kayak and rafting trips, including full moon tours.

Snapshots of Shenandoah National Park and Luray Caverns

Luray Caverns

970 U.S. Highway, 211 West, Luray, 540-743-6551; www.luraycaverns.com
Beneath the mountains of Virginia lie countless caverns where dark narrow passages lead to hidden dangers: shear cliffs, treacherous muddy slopes and raging underground rivers. But caves are also places of immense beauty—rooms the size of cathedrals filled with stalactites, stalagmites and amazing natural artworks. You don't, however, have to slither on your belly like a snake or cram your body through a rocky crevice to enjoy this world within our world. You can stroll right through the largest and most popular cavern in Eastern America—Luray Caverns. An hour-long tour through the cave system follows a figure-eight path with views of formations that resemble towering columns, fried eggs and intricate draperies. The tour includes a melodious interlude of the song "Oh, Shenandoah" on what could be the world's largest musical instrument, the Great Stalacpipe Organ, which is composed of stalactites from over three acres within the cavern. The highlight is Giant's Hall, a 17-story tall underground chamber with formations so massive and colorful it's almost cartoon-like. Luray Caverns also features an antique car museum and a garden maze made from 1,500 eight-foot-tall Dark American Arbovitae trees. A half-mile long pathway within the maze consists of forty spots where a choice is needed to solve the puzzle. Tours begin each day at 9 a.m.

VIRGINIA WINE COUNTRY

Shenandoah National Park
540-999-3500; www.nps.gov/shen
The 197,411-acre park near the inn is famous for having more than 500 miles of hiking trails and the amazing 105-mile-long Skyline Drive, a picturesque drive along the ridge top with 75 scenic overlooks. The park was enacted in 1926 by Congress as part of a greater effort to preserve national treasures with the creation of the National Park Service. SNP is a habitat that contains 100 species of trees, 200 species of birds and 1,100 varieties of plants, as well as countless species of wildlife. The park was completed in 1936 and dedicated by Franklin D. Roosevelt. While most of the park remained undeveloped during its history, a desire to further protect it occurred in 1976 when Congress designated 79,019 acres as officially protected wilderness, with an additional 500 acres added under the Wilder Preservation System in 1978. The combination of wilderness and non-wilderness areas allows visitors to experience SNP in a wide variety of ways. In addition to the over 500 miles of hiking trails, rock climbing instruction and a variety of ranger-led nature programs are available. The SNP entry fee is $8 per person or $15 per vehicle. For rock climbing, visit www.visitshenandoah.com or call 888-896-3833.

see
Hiking
Looking for the perfect day hike? More than 100,000 people hike Shenandoah's 3,291-foot-tall Old Rag Mountain every year. The 7.1-mile circuit hike (plus 0.9 miles each way from the parking area to the trail head) generally takes 5 to 7 hours at a leisurely pace. Offset from the main ridge in Shenandoah National Park, the rocky summit provides a panoramic view of the valleys, foothills and farmland around the park as well as the peaks on Skyline Drive, Robertson Mountain, Crescent Rocks and Spitler Hill. In the spring, the trail winds through dense rows of white and pink Mountain Laurels. In the summer, the haze against the thick forest gives the Blue Ridge Mountains their blue color. In the fall, the foliage radiates in brilliant

yellows and fiery reds. The pathway climbs above the tree line and requires some rock scrambling over boulders and up and down rock walls to reach the summit. Because it is such a popular climb, avoid it on weekends during the fall if you want a serene experience.

Llama trekking

Llamas are thought to be more sure-footed and personable than other pack animals and make hiking accessible to those who are disinclined or unable to haul cumbersome gear themselves: Llamas will carry books, binoculars and anything else you'd like to bring along. Springtime and early summer treks feature bird-watching and wildflower identification sessions (treks are not available during the hot summer days from the end of June to early August.) A trek begins with an introduction to each of the llamas and a lesson on how to lead them. **Twincreeks Llamas** (*427 Turtle Lane, Brownton, 540-631-9175; www.twincreeksllamas.com*) offers a variety of two-hour and half-day llama treks in Shenandoah River State Park and the George Washington National Forest.

SHENANDOAH NATIONAL PARK

Horseback riding

Why walk when you can ride? Virginia is, after all, horse country. The **Marriott Ranch** (*5305 Marriott Lane, Hume*) of the Old West conducts 90 minute guided trail rides for non-riders as well as longer rides, such as dinner and breakfast rides, into the mountains and along the Shenandoah River. Experienced riders may wish to join one of the full day cattle drives held three times per year. **Lantern Lane Farms** (*16 Lantern Lane, Viewtown, 800-360-3831; www.lanternlanefarm.com*) offers group and private riding instruction and guided trail rides to riders able to walk and trot. An evaluation ride is required for all trail rides.

Wine tasting

Washington is conveniently located within a short drive of a half dozen vineyards. In addition to Gray Ghost and Unicorn, try **Pearmund Cellars Winery** (*6190 Georgetown Road, Broad Run, 540-347-3475; www.pearmundcellars.com; daily 10 a.m.-6 p.m.*) The vineyard has been in operation for over 20 years and is located on a 100-acre farm that dates back to 1743. Pearmund is one of the few American wineries that make a malbec, a common South American varietal. Taste a little bit of old European charm

MARRIOTT RANCH

with traditional winemaking methods at **Smokehouse Winery** (*10 Ashby Road, Sperryville, 540-987-3194; www.smokehousewinery.com; open February-December, weekends noon-6 p.m.*). The winery specializes in meads (honey wines) with more than a half dozen varieties. After a long hike, stop in at **Sharp Rock** (*5 Sharp Rock Road, Sperryville, 540-987-8020; www.sharprock-vineyards.com; open mid-February-December, Friday through Sunday from 11 a.m.-5 p.m.*), conveniently located at the base of Old Rag Mountain. The tasting fee is $2. One of the premier vineyards is **Oasis** (*12507 Lee Highway, Washington, 540-635-3103; www.oasiswine.com; Open Monday-Friday 11 a.m.-5 p.m.; Weekends 11 a.m.-6 p.m.*), which features a wide assortment of reds, whites and champagnes. The vineyard has a grand tasting area with two decks, one looking out at the mountains. The Brut is rated one of the best sparkling wines in the world. An introductory tasting costs $5.

ANOTHER BRIGHT IDEA

A great way to visit several of the vineyards and not worry about driving is with **Virginia Wine Country Tours** (*540-622-2505; www.virginiawinecountrytours.com*), which provides limousine wine tours starting at $70 per hour. All tours are customized and generally include pick-up, drop off and stops at 3-5 vineyards.

drive

Instead of heading directly back along the same route, take a detour into historic Front Royal, Virginia via Route 211 West to route 522 North. The town is another fine example of a historic main street in Virginia, with numerous antique shops, galleries and specialty stores. A great stop is at **Vintage Swank** (*212 East Main St., 540-636-0069; www.vintageswank.com*). The store sells an assortment of quirky items from the past and not so distant past: Art Deco knickknacks, phones with dials, Lucite purses, old denim and Leprechaun-printed towels. From Front Royal, it's a straight shot back on I-66 to the capital city.

index

SUNRISE AT KIAWAH ISLAND GOLF RESORT

GOLDEN GATE BRIDGE

NAPA VALLEY VINEYARDS

SEATTLE SPACE NEEDLE

art credits

Illustrations
All illustrated maps: ©Jennifer Thermes

Chapter 1: Boston to the Berkshires
Boston Harbor: *Greater Boston Convention and Visitors Bureau*
Boston Harbor Hotel
Four Seasons Hotel Boston
Garden at the Mount: *Berkshire Visitors Bureau/Gardens at the Mount/Kevin Sprague*
Picture Book Art Museum: *The Eric Carle Museum of Picture Book Art/Paul Shoul*
Church at Lenox: *Berkshire Visitors Bureau/Steve Ziglar*
Cheshire Lake in Summer: *Berkshire Visitors Bureau/Ann Claffie*
Cheshire Foliage: *Berkshire Visitors Bureau/Ann Claffie*
Kripalu Blossoms: *Berkshire Visitors Bureau/Ann Claffie*
Blantyre House: Bluebbery Pancake, Ice House Guest Room, Porch, Pool:
Wheatleigh: View of the Berkshires, Front of House, Dining Room, Great Hall, Lobster Dish, Terrace Suite
Kripalu: *Berkshire Visitors Bureau/Kripalu*
Dalton: *Berkshire Visitors Bureau/Ann Claffie*
The Mount: *Berkshire Visitors Bureau/David Dashiell*

Chapter 2: Denver to Aspen
Aspen Summer Lake: *Aspen Chamber Resort Association/Daniel Bayer*
Colorado River Run: *Colorado Tourism Office/ Matt Inden/Weaver Multi Media Group*
Frisco: *Mark Fox*
Aspen Town Summer: *Aspen Chamber Resort Association/Daniel Bayer*
Vail Foliage: *Colorado Tourism Office/Matt Inden/Weaver Multi Media Group*
Cycling: *Colorado Tourism Office/ Matt Inden/Weaver Multi Media Group*

CARMEL CITY BEACH

The Ritz Bachelor Gulch Edwards: *Colorado Tourism Office/ Matt Inden/Weaver Multi Media Group*
Summer Aspen: *Aspen Chamber Resort Association/Burnham W. Arndt*
Skiing at Beaver Creek: *Vail Resorts*
The St Regis Aspen Winter Exterior Aspen: *Colorado Tourism Office/ Matt Inden/Weaver Multi Media Group*
Little Nell Aspen Bathroom Suite
St Regis Aspen View
Little Nell Aspen Bedroom
Aspen Maroon Bells Summer: *Aspen Chamber Resort Association/ Daniel Bayer*

Chapter 3: Los Angeles to La Jolla
Peninsula Hotel Beverly Hills Pool
California Route 1: *1997 California Division of Tourism/Robert Holmes*
Boats in Newport Harbor: *Newport Beach Conference and Visitors Bureau*
Fairmont Newport Beach Bedroom
Balboa Pier: Newport Beach Conference and Visitors Bureau
The Island Hotel Patio
Fairmont Hotel Rooftop Pool
Newport Beach Harbor: *Newport Beach Conference and Visitors Bureau*
The Island Hotel Pool and Spa
Five Crowns Restaurant: *Newport Beach Conference and Visitors Bureau*
Corona Del Mar Beach: *Newport Beach Conference and Visitors Bureau*

Torrey Pines State Reserve: *San Diego Convention and Visitors Bureau/ Joanne DiBona*
The Lodge at Torrey Pines: Pool and Lodge
Laurel Bar
Laurel Restaurant
Jack's La Jolla
Scripps Cove La Jolla: *San Diego Convention and Visitors Bureau/Joanne DiBona*
Gas lamp Quarter: *San Diego Convention and Visitors Bureau/ Joanne DiBona*
Pacific Beach: *San Diego Convention and Visitors Bureau/Joanne DiBona*
Del Mar Beach: *San Diego Convention and Visitors Bureau/ Joanne DiBona*
Ocean Beach: *San Diego Convention and Visitors Bureau/Joanne DiBona*
Pacific Beach: *San Diego Convention and Visitors Bureau/Joanne DiBona*

Chapter 4: Los Angeles to Santa Barbara
Hotel Bel-Air Beverly Hills
Four Seasons Santa Barbara
Bacara Resort and Spa Swimming Pool, Bacara Resort Fitness Trail
San Ysidro Ranch Exterior, Outdoor Dining, Bath, Four Poster
Elements Restaurant Appetizer
Spa Entrance at the Four Seasons

Olio e Limone Walnut Salad
Bacara Spa at Night
Santa Barbara Botanic Garden
Meadow: *Santa Barbara Botanic Garden*
Santa Barbara Farmer's Market: *Santa Barbara Conference and Visitors Bureau and Film Commission*
Mission Santa Barbara Garden's: *Santa Barbara Conference and Visitors Bureau amd Film Commission*
Lake Cachuma Santa Ynez: *Santa Barbara Conference and Visitors Bureau and Film Commission*
Stearns Wharf: *Santa Barbara Conference and Visitors Bureau and Film Commission*
Mission Santa Barbara: *Santa Barbara Conference and Visitors Bureau and Film Commission*

Chapter 5: Nashville to Asheville
Hermitage Hotel: Nashville Room, Capitol Grille, Foyer
Nashville Music Hall of Fame: *Nashville Convention and Visitors Bureau*
Nashville River: *Nashville Convention and Visitors Bureau*
Blackberry Farm Fishing, Horses, Boating, Cycling: *Beall and Thomas Photography*
Blackberry Farm: *Beall and Thomas Photography*
Asheville: *North Carolina Tourism/ Bill Russ*
Tupelo Honey Café: *Steven McBride Photography, Inc*
Inn at Biltmore Estate: Guest room
Conservatory Rose Garden: *2007 The Biltmore Company, all rights reserved*
Lagoon View: *2007 The Biltmore Company, all rights reserved*
Inn at Biltmore: Arial View with Pool
Shrub Garden: *2007 The Biltmore Company, all rights reserved*
Winter Garden: *2007 The Biltmore Company, all rights reserved*
Summer on the Lake: *2007 The Biltmore Company, all rights reserved*

Chapter 6: New York to Newport
Brooklyn Bridge: *NYC and Company/ Jeff Greenberg*
Mandarin Oriental Hotel New York: Hudson Bathroom, Central Park View, Hudson Bedroom
Newport Coast: *Onne Van Der Wal/ www.vanderwal.com*
Wine Bar at the Griswold Inn: *Peter Paige*
Sailboat Passing Castle Hill Inn: *Onne Van Der Wal/www.vanderwal.com*
The Chanler at Cliff Walk, The Chanler Bedroom, The Chanler at Cliff Walk: *Simone Ink*
Castle Hill Inn, Castle Hill Inn Bedroom, Castle Hill Dining Room: *Relais and Chateaux*
Fluke Wine Bar and Kitchen
Newport Harbour: *Onne Van Der Wal/www.vanderwal.com*
Marble House: *John Corbett/The Preservation Society of Newport County*
Fort Adams: *Newport RI Visitors Bureau*
Marble House Dining Room: *Preservation Society of Newport County*

Chapter 7: San Diego to Laguna
Laguna Beach: St. Regis Monarch
St. Regis Monarch: Rotunda Staircase, Ocean Pool View Vivace Restaurant
St. Regis Monarch: Pool Entrance, Terrace, Fountain
Veranda at the Ritz Carlton Laguna Niguel
The Montage Hotel and Coastline, Balcony Views at the Montage, Studio Restaurant, Cabana's at Montage
Stonehill Tavern
Spa Montage
Spa Gaucin at the St. Regis
Laguna Beach Lifeguard Tower
Sapphire Laguna Restaurant
Ritz Carlton Laguna Niguel Spa

ART CREDITS

Chapter 8: San Francisco to The Napa Valley
St Regis Hotel San Francisco Pool
San Francisco Skyline: *SFCVB/Lewis Sommer*
San Francisco Victorian Houses: *SFCVB/Phillip H.Coblentz*
San Francisco Cable Car: *SFCVB/Phillip H. Coblentz*
Napa Valley: *www.winecountry.com*
Calistoga Ranch Pool
Napa Valley: *Brent Miller/Winecountry.com*
Calistoga Ranch Dining
Calistoga: *Calistoga Chamber of Commerce*
Calistoga Bathouse
Ca' Toga Galleria D'art
Woodhouse Chocolate
Meadowood Napa Valley
Auberge Du Soleil at Dusk, Scallops at Auberge Du Soleil, Auberge Du Soleil Spa Loungers
The French Laundry Yountville, The French Laundry Dining Room
Dining Room and Bar at Bouchon
Napa Valley Opera House Exterior, Stairs: *David Wakely*
COPIA
Castello Di Amorosa
Sonoma Vineyards: *Robert Janover/www.sonomacounty.com*

Chapter 9: San Francisco to Oakhurst
Sun Sun Wo: Mariposa *County Visitors Bureau/Leroy Radanovich*
Downtown Mariposa: *Mariposa Country Visitors Bureau/Leroy Radanovich*
Coulterville: *Mariposa County Visitors Bureay/Leroy Radanovich*
Oakdale Cowboy Museum
Chateau de Sureau: *Dr. William Clanin*
Erna's Elderberry Restaurant: *Dr. William Clanin*
Spa du Sureau: *Dr. William Clanin*
Lake McClure: *Mariposa County Visitors Bureau/Leroy Radanovich*
Half Dome Sunset: *Yosemite National Park/Mariposa County Visitors Bureau/Leroy Radanovich*
Bay Bridge: *SFCVB/Phillip H. Coblentz*
Merced River Cathedral Rocks: *Yosemite National Park/Mariposa County Visitors Bureau/Leroy Radanovich*

Chapter 10: San Jose to Big Sur
Carmel by the Sea: Scenic Road in Carmel, Cottage, Dolores Street Shops, Point Lobos
Bernardus Lodge Vineyard, Outdoor Spa, Grounds
Spa at Quail Lodge: *Monterey County CVB*
Garden Salad at Marinus Restaurant
Big Sur Coastline: *©istockphoto.com/Aimin Tang*
View From the Post Ranch Inn: *Post Ranch Inn/Larry Dale Gordon*
Sunset Exterior, Sierra Mar Restaurant, Infinity Pool at the Post Ranch Inn Spa: *Post ranch Inn/Kodiak Greenwood*
Prawns at Cielo Restaurant
Big Sur Coastline: *©istockphoto.com/Dana Blankenship*
McWay Falls: *Monterey County CVB*
Hearst Castle: *Hearst Castle/California State Parks*

Chapter 11: Savannah to Charleston and Kiawah
The Beach at Kiawah Island Sunset: Kiawah Island Golf Resort
The Battery: Charleston Area CVB/www.charlestoncvb.com
The Planters Inn
The Charleston Place Hotel Pool
Wentworth Mansion
The Charleston Place Guest Room
High Cotton Exterior
Slightly North of Board Crab Cakes
Slightly North of Board Interior
Historic Carriage Tours: *Charleston Area CVB/www.charlestoncvb.com*
Rainbow Row: Charleston Area CVB
Nathaniel Russell House Garden

TORREY PINES STATE RESERVE

Magnolia Plantation: *Charleston Area CVB/www.charlestoncvb.com*
Fort Sumter
Nathaniel Russell House Staircase: *Rick Rhodes*
Nathaniel Russell House Exterior: *Bill Struhs*
Kiawah Island Golf Resort: Ocean Course, Sanctuary Lobby bar, Beach Umbrella, Sanctuary Pool, Sanctuary Corner Suite,
Flying Heron, Sunset on the Golf Course, Sanctuary Morning Room, Ocean Room Dining

Chapter 12: Seattle to Vancouver
Sutton Place Hotel Wine Merchant, Grand Suite
Four Seasons Vancouver Pool, Dining Room, Guest room
Sweet Obsession: Signature Wedding Cake
West Dining Room
Lumiere Restaurant
Vancouver Art Gallery: *Vancouver Art Gallery/Tomas Svab*
Jellyfish: *Vancouver Aquarium/Neil Fisher*
Four Seasons Resort Whistler Poolside
Outdoor Activities and Dining at Four Seasons Resort Whistler

Whistler Blakcomb: *©istockphoto. com/John Pitcher*
Whistler Blackcomb Village
Desert at Araxi Restaurant

Chapter 13: Washington to Washington
Washington Monument: *Washington DC Convention and Tourism Corporation*
The Inn at Little Washington
Fall Colors in Washington VA: *Washington VA/Kevin Adams*
Handmade Gifts at R.H. Ballard
The Inn at Little Washington: Duck Dish, Claiborne House, A Guestroom, The Inn at Dusk, Veranda, Sorrel and Caviar
Shenandoah National Park
Butterfly: *National Park Service Photo*
Luray Caverns: *Luray Caverns/ National Parks*
Shenandoah Chipmunk: *National Park Service Photo*
Shenandoah Fall in White Oak Canyon: *National Park Service Photo*
Virginia Wine Country: *Keith Lanpher/VTC*
Shenandoah Old Rag Mountain: *National Park Service Photo*
Marriott Ranch: Marriott *Ranch/ Tommy McMillan*

Index